475 SOUTH SEAWARD
VENTURA, CA 93003

MAKING A MESS AND MEETING GOD

Unruly Ideas and Everyday Experiments for Worship

MANDY SMITH

Standard® PUBLISHING

Cincinnati, Ohio

Published by Standard Publishing, Cincinnati, Ohio
www.standardpub.com

Printed in: United States of America

Project editor: Laura Derico
Cover art and design: Scott Ryan
Interior design: Katherine Lloyd, The DESK

ISBN 978-0-7847-2392-0

Library of Congress Cataloging-in-Publication Data
Smith, Mandy, 1971-
  Making a mess and meeting God : unruly ideas and everyday experiments for worship / Mandy Smith.
      p. cm.
  Includes bibliographical references (p.   ) and indexes.
  ISBN 978-0-7847-2392-0 (perfect bound)
 1. Christian life--Textbooks. 2. Christian education--Textbooks for adults. I. Title.
  BV4511.S655 2010
  248.4--dc22
                          2010009252
15 14 13 12 11 10   1 2 3 4 5 6 7 8 9

To the mess-makers at my house.

—M. S.

"What I am here describing as imagination in its highest form
is more properly to be called faith."
—Edward Robinson, *The Language of Mystery*

"I devoted myself to study and to explore . . ."
—Ecclesiastes 1:13

A portion of the proceeds of this book will go to
La Armonia Hermosa, a coffee co-op,
helping to provide a living wage and fair-trade opportunities
www.laarmoniahermosa.com

Contents

TALKING AND THINKING OUR WAY TO GOD

"That which was from the beginning, which we have heard, which we have seen with our eyes, which we have looked at and our hands have touched—this we proclaim concerning the Word of life."
—1 JOHN 1:1

The words "and now, as we turn to a time of Communion" made my pulse race. I have to confess that, in the early years of my faith, Communion stressed me out. As soon as the Communion meditation began, I knew the clock was running—by the time I sipped the juice, I had to be in a state of perfect emotional and spiritual alignment with God. This meant that I had about three minutes to put aside all the thoughts I'd been thinking all week, focus on some otherworldly truth, and have an emotional and spiritual response to that truth. This required an investment of an incredible force of mental and spiritual energy, and most weeks I just didn't have it. Sometimes I could manage the first stage of clearing my mind of distractions, but rarely did I achieve the ultimate desired state by the time the amen was said. When I finally became aware of the pressure I felt to fathom deep truths in a short period of time, I decided to opt out and just take Communion.

And then a funny thing happened. As I broke the bread, my fingertips got truth. As I let it crumble in my mouth, my teeth got truth. As I lifted my arm to drink, my muscles got truth. And my mind followed.

The saying goes, "Where the mind leads, the body will follow," and there is certainly something to be said for that. However, directing a mind to spiritual things, especially in an age of crammed schedules, pinging e-mails, and clamoring advertisements, takes superhuman quantities of determination and focus. How are we supposed to have the quiet and energy required for all that mental control? No wonder devotion becomes drudgery and worship just feels like work. Are we still children of the Enlightenment, subconsciously following Descartes's "I think, therefore I am"? Of course, thinking is good, but is it the only way to discover God? Or could we interpret Jesus' words in John 14:21, "Whoever has my commands and obeys them, he is the one who loves me," to mean instead, "I do, therefore I am"? (But not in the I-do-good-things-therefore-I-have-worked-my-way-into-heaven sense.) Jesus seems to say that when we worship God with our lives and actions, we worship God with our hearts. Doing reveals our love, but maybe it also deepens it. This switches the old adage: Where the body leads, the mind will follow.

So what does that look like? As I read my own words "where the body leads, the mind will follow," even I have fears that it means doing weird things in the name of getting out of comfort zones to have some kind of artificial, multisensory, supernatural experience. But this is not where I'm headed at all. My point is simply about discovering the potential that ordinary activities and daily life have to teach us about God in a new and deeper way, not for the sake of an experience alone, but for the sake of seeing and knowing God on a new level. Our efforts to comprehend and connect with God usually involve so many words—reading, praying, journaling, listening, talking, thinking, singing. Can we add to these the possibility of learning and connecting through holding, shaping, walking, sitting, standing, making, and doing?

"Evangelical Christians are over-cognitive, meaning that we over-rely on this aspect of humanness to define our Christianity."

—Dr. Tom Thompson, psychologist (said in conversation)

We want very much to have a practical life application of all we learn at church, in our small groups and in our personal Bible study. Perhaps a practical application would flow more naturally if our hands and feet were involved in the learning process. A child might chant "two minus one is one" all day long in class, but when he has two gummy bears in his hand and he drops one, he fathoms that reality in a new way. A music student might read every paper ever written about Bach's Toccata and Fugue in D Minor, and be able to explain every diminished seventh chord and arpeggio, but when she can play it, then she really understands it, right down to her fingertips. We may study every geographical feature of the Grand Canyon, but when we scramble up its sides, and have the scraped knees to prove it, its truth becomes ours.

It is the hope of all Christians and all church leaders that we, and those we teach, may not just say "I know about God" but "I've met God." How can we go beyond the cognitive level of talking about God to meet him in a real and deep way? Words are good for passing on truth, but they're not the only way. God didn't only *describe* the creation he had imagined, he *formed* it. Jesus didn't only *say* "I love you," he *lived* it (and died it). We can most certainly get truth through our ears, but we underestimate the ways we can get it through our eyes and nerves and even through our muscles. I could spend ten minutes calming my frightened child with dry words—"Now, now, it's not so bad. You'll feel better soon." But if I lift him into a warm bath, then pick him up and wrap him in a blue towel, I might reach parts of his mind and soul my words could never touch. His eyes and nerves and muscles would comprehend calm while his ears were still processing all the talk.

How can we plug into such a powerful tool in our personal spiritual lives and in the lives of our churches? How can we know, and help others know, old truths in more meaningful ways? These are the questions we're about to explore. When I explained these ideas to a friend who is a first-grade teacher, her eyes lit up. "We use object lessons all the time with kids," she said. "But kids often miss the abstract side of the lesson. Grown-ups would get them so much more." So think of this book as a collection of object lessons for grown-ups.

In the pages that follow, our exploration will take two main forms.

"KNEEL

and

PRAY

and

YOU

will

BELIEVE."

—*attributed to Blaise Pascal, mathematician, physicist, and philosopher*

> "Practice is to Judaism what belief is to Christianity. That is not to say that Judaism doesn't have dogma or doctrine. It is rather to say that for Jews, the essence of the thing is a doing, an action. Your faith might come and go, but your practice ought not waver. (Indeed, Judaism suggests that the repeating of the practice is the best way to ensure that a doubter's faith will return.)"
>
> —LAUREN WINNER, *Mudhouse Sabbath: An Invitation to a Life of Spiritual Discipline*

First, we'll develop a dogged determination to find God in every moment, every activity of our days. When we sense God is with us as we walk, we have walked with God. When we are grateful for the color of our spouse's eyes, we have seen God's beauty. We will be able to fathom our Father and his creation in a myriad of new ways and say "I've met God."

Second, we'll explore through dabbling in a little art. Now before all the "creatively challenged" disengage, let me explain. No one considers how well they sing before belting out Broadway tunes in the bathtub. Singing belongs to the gifted and the ungifted, the professional and the amateur alike. Sadly, though, for many of us, art fell out of our experience the ninety-seventh time we heard "What *is* it?" There is a fear associated with being asked to make something and it is usually expressed with these words: "I'm not very good at art." But this is not about *good* art. This is about a playful exploration of the basic design principles God set into his creation. This is a chance to reflect in the outer world what we carry in our inner world.

It's only right to begin an experiment with a hypothesis, so here's mine. If we explore these new opportunities to find the divine in the ordinary and through a little artful play, then we will discover new depths in our comprehension of and communication with God. But since what we're going to try is a little different from the ways twenty-first-century, Western, evangelical Christians usually learn and worship, we'll also give ourselves a little time to ponder—in short essays called the "Elements of Making and Meeting." As we do the experiments that follow, we'll take with us the messages from these essays: learning to enjoy the process, to value ritual, quality, and metaphor, and to see the special in the ordinary.

When we're done, we'll know a little better how to slow down. We'll rediscover the relationship between our bodies and our souls and our world. We will be more whole and more present and more happy. We'll be more in touch with each other, and with God. And we might even have a little FUN.

DROP CLOTHS ON THE CEILING—
PREPARING FOR THE MESS

*"A good shoe is a shoe you don't notice. Good reading becomes possible when
you need not consciously think about eyes, or light, or print, or spelling.
The perfect church service would be one we were almost unaware of;
our attention would have been on God."*

—C. S. LEWIS, *LETTERS TO MALCOLM: CHIEFLY ON PRAYER*

Experimentation can be scary. It may take us to unexplored territory or explode in our faces. It may teach us difficult lessons or just make a big mess. For some, the new and unknown is exciting, but for others, it's distracting or even intimidating. So to get the point of these experiments, first we need to face a few fears. To release ourselves to playfulness, we need to loosen up a little.

Let's start by looking at two important issues: how to open ourselves to creativity and how to prepare experiments for the tricky dynamics of a group setting. The point is to focus on God, not on our own discomfort. Read on to discover how to create environments conducive to devotion, rather than distraction, to creativity, rather than anxiety. To adapt the quote from C. S. Lewis, the perfect worship experiment would be one we were almost unaware of; our attention would have been on God.

Permission to Make a Mess

Our parents have taught us so well to be neat that it takes a little while to overcome that instinct. Watching my kids, I've learned that tidiness and creativity rarely coexist, and I've gradually resigned myself to the fact. But after years of training in tidiness, the average adult needs a lot of permission to be experimental—permission to take a long time and make a big mess, permission to do it our own way or in our own space. And definitely permission for it to not look great. So say this—or something like it—to yourself or to your group before beginning:

Remember when you were a kid and there was an opportunity to finger-paint? Did you stress about how it would look or how much mess it would make? Or would you squeal "Ooo! Green!" and go for it? Here is your chance to reconnect with that adventurous and experimental spirit. The point here is not how it looks, but how the act of making something helps you process the ideas in your head and the feelings in your heart. The end product will be an internal one, helped along by this external process. So start with a few minutes to pray or read over your notes or just sit in silence to remember the ideas we've been studying. When you feel ready, gather your materials, find a comfortable spot, and make a MESS.

AWAKENING PLAYFULNESS

How many people do you know who happily call themselves "artists"? I have a drawer filled with art supplies and a house full of things I've made, and other people call me an artist, but I still have a hard time using the word for myself. I think it's because you can say "I'm a diver" or "I'm a mechanic" and it just means "I do diving" or "I do mechanics." But for some reason, when you say "I'm an artist" it's like saying "I make art—and it's good!" But when I'm staring at a blank page, I don't know yet if what I'm about to do is good. And if it's not going to be good, then what's the point in even starting? Making something out of nothing can be intimidating—the pressure of invisible critics makes the maker incredibly self-conscious. Starting is half the hurdle. So, how do we start?

You may be pleased to find that you've already started. Even if you don't regularly make art or go to art galleries, you are more involved in art than you realize. **You know a secret language which you may not know you know.** Artists call it the "elements of design" but we're all fluent in its vocabulary of line, shape, direction, size, texture, and color. From an early age, we have learned from nature to make certain connections between how a thing looks and what it is—something rounded is likely to be soft, something red could be hot.

Trouble is, we learned these connections so long ago that we are no longer conscious of them. We interpret images (whether they're works of art, human faces, or advertisements) without even being aware of the interpretation process. We find ourselves reaching for the remote every time a particular ad comes on or wanting to rest our eyes on a particular face. We just don't usually stop to dissect how we interpreted those images, why they made us feel the way they did.

So we're not about to step into a new world of art, after all. We're simply moving to the role of active creator—speaking the language we already know—instead of (seemingly) passive interpreter. To do this, we have to stop and **think about the connections and interpretations we make every day.** We need to become familiar with the vocabulary we'll be using and the choices we'll be making.

Exercises to melt self-consciousness and awaken PLAYFULNESS:

- In a book or online, find pictures of *Peace Window* by Marc Chagall (www.peacewindow.org) and *Guernica* by Pablo Picasso (you can even explore the painting in 3–D at www.lena-gieseke.com/guernica/movie.html or on YouTube). Look at the lines and colors chosen by the artists. What makes one artwork feel peaceful and one disturbing?

- Consider what choices you would make to communicate various atmospheres by connecting words on the right with words on the left in the chart on the side of this page (there may be many right answers).

IF A SHAPE OR LINE IS:	I INTERPRET IT AS:
Black	Natural
Angular	Eye-catching
White	Reassuring
Jagged	Cold
Smooth	Hopeful
Horizontal	Evil
Square	Uncomfortable
Light	Hot
Thin	Frightening
Round	Cruel
Yellow	Good
Bright	Pure
Blotchy	Sickly
Pink	Disturbing
Dark	Pleasant
Vertical	Alive
Rough	Festive
Triangular	Fresh
Lumpy	Dangerous
Blue	Unpleasant
Diagonal	Calming
Green	Warm
Muted	Fun

IF I WANT TO COMMUNICATE:	I COULD USE THESE SHAPES/ LINES/COLORS (draw or describe them):
Confusion	
Happiness	
Depression	
Peace	

- Now try working in the opposite direction: use the chart on this page to think about what shapes/lines/colors you would use to communicate certain feelings or concepts. Fill in your own ideas.

- Draw something very simple such as a tree or a stick man with your non-dominant hand. Is that hard to do? Does it feel strange? Are you more conscious of the process of drawing?

- Finger-paint or scribble aimlessly. Don't think too much about what it will look like, just follow your instincts and choose colors and lines purely because you feel like it. What is your favorite part of your creation? Why?

- What do you think would be the color blue's favorite shape? Take a blue pencil and find out.

- Squirt a few blobs of paint in various colors (acrylic or poster paints work best) on a sheet of paper, then fold it in half. Squish it flat and then open it to see what has happened with the paint. Did it create some interesting patterns or maybe even recognizable shapes? What are they?

- Randomly choose two pictures from a magazine (if you're doing this in a group setting, provide a random selection of images cut from magazines, not the entire magazine) and then consider ways they are similar. For example, a bird and a refrigerator could be said to be similar because they both use air, they both make a high-pitched noise, or because they both contain eggs. A corncob and a human head could be similar because they both grow, they both need sunshine, or they both have ears! There are no wrong answers (although some may be more "corny" than others).

- Look at children's books about art: *Take a Look: An Introduction to the Experience of Art*, by Rosemary Davidson; *The Art Pack*, by Christophe Frayling, Helen Frayling, Ron Van Der Meer; *Ish*, by Peter H. Reynolds.

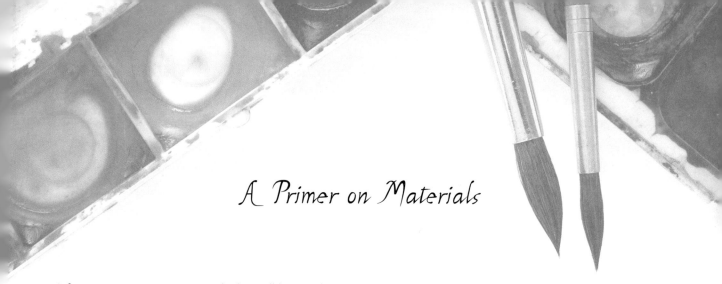

A Primer on Materials

A few tips on common materials that will be used in our experiments: while all of these items are available in art stores, if you're on a tight budget, I would suggest trying a craft store (such as Michael's Craft or Hobby Lobby). For online shopping, www.Jerrysartarama.com and www.misterart.com also have great sales on art supplies.

Stretched canvas

This is the traditional artist's canvas—white canvas fabric stapled onto a wooden frame—which can come in many different shapes and sizes. These can get expensive so look for them on sale or in bulk.

Canvas board

A cheaper alternative to the stretched canvas, canvas boards are made by applying canvas to a piece of board. Again, they come in many sizes.

Be creative in gathering background materials. If the experiment requires a flat background like a canvas, could you use an old door? an old game board? a tray? a discarded dresser drawer? See what you can find in dumpsters, attics, thrift stores. Something which already has its own story might add an interesting element to your art. Just be sure it's clean—a greasy surface won't accept paint. And check that it will take the paint you're using—it may need sanding or stripping if it has a coat of polyurethane or glossy paint.

Paint

I find that the easiest paint to use is acrylic paint. It's available in bottles in craft stores, is quite affordable, and washes out with water. The bottled acrylic paint covers quite well and has a satisfying depth of color, but if you want a step up, try Liquitex acrylics, which come in tubes and are more expensive. They wash in water but have a buttery texture, like oil paint. On the other hand, if you have old cans of house paint lying around, they would work as well.

Paintbrushes

If you can, try to use brushes with nice bristles (not plastic bristles or sponge brushes). While brushes can get expensive, you can buy inexpensive sets of brushes of assorted sizes and shapes, and with natural or synthetic hair bristles, for under $10.

When using paint, it's also a good idea to have palettes (plastic container lids work fine), water bowls, rags or paper towels, and drop cloths on hand.

CROWD CONTROL, OR NOT:
ADAPTATIONS FOR WORSHIP OR GROUP SETTINGS

Worship planners love to talk about, and challenge, comfort zones. While there's no doubt that bridging the gap between our physical world and an unseen God requires a bit of a stretch, not all discomfort in worship is necessarily a sign that we're overcoming our resistance to God. Sometimes what a worship leader would call "getting out of your comfort zone so you can be open to God" could otherwise be called "overriding normal social and cultural mores to the point of embarrassment and distraction in the name of worship." Experiments can be effective in worship services and group settings but I've also seen them done in ways that are forced and uncomfortable. Unless they're done with a little care, they can accomplish the exact opposite of their intended purpose, drawing the worshiper's attention to their own bare feet, rather than to God. All of the experiments in this book are first presented for individual use, then adaptations are suggested for group settings. But there are some additional ways to make them especially effective for a group, so let's quickly consider a few important issues.

If I am an "I"

Since experimentation becomes a personal expression of the inner soul of the worshiper, you may find that those who are more introverted don't want to expose that inner soul to a large group. And, if creating is a way to process an idea, some need to do that alone. They may be ready to share their ideas once they've had the time to put them in order. Is there a way to allow space or time for some to begin the experiment alone or at home?

Don't rush me!

Creativity, sadly, can be a timid and fickle creature. Like a cat, it wants to approach when it's good and ready and stay not a moment more, or less, than it likes. Is it possible to give people some notice of the project so they have time to think about it before having to create? Or break the project down into smaller parts to spread it out over several meetings? Most of my artworks take weeks to create in my imagination and only days to create with my hands. Some group experiments will take more time and preparation than the average worship service allows (or need to be adapted to fit a worship service setting) and so may lend themselves more to a family, small group, community, or retreat setting. Do people feel unrushed in the creative process?

"This world is but a canvas to our imaginations."

—Henry David Thoreau,
A Week on the Concord and Merrimack Rivers

It don't mean a thing

For many, those elements that "work" (in that they draw attention to spiritual matters and not to themselves or the person doing them) in corporate worship often work because they're familiar. Without dissecting the role of ritual, it's enough to say that if we came to the table for Christmas dinner to find a foot-long chili dog instead of a turkey or ham, it just wouldn't feel right, no matter how much it was festooned with cranberries. Turkeys and their trimmings are meaningful because we've had them before—they bring to mind many years of experiences. The same goes for worship. If someone has never made something in order to worship, it may not hold that meaning for him, at least not at first.

Is This Experiment Right for My Group?

Here are some questions to ask yourself (if you are a group leader) or your group members, if appropriate:

1. Do those in the group feel safe? Do they trust others in the group enough to express themselves openly?

2. Is the group too large to allow a feeling of safety? Would breaking out into smaller spaces or groups help?

3. Have those in the group had time to pray and reflect in order to know what they want to express to God? Would it be helpful/possible for a description of the project to be provided in advance so individuals can prepare for it?

4. Could the group be given small-group discussion time and/or private reflection time in order to prepare themselves for the experiment?

5. How long will the process take (without rushing our creators)?

6. What materials will be required (for the project but also for preparation and cleanup)?

7. What could go wrong? How can you plan to avoid it or prepare for it?

8. Is the space appropriate?

9. Will the group complete a project together or will they work on individual projects? Working on individual projects means that, for a rather personal subject, people can express very private thoughts yet still be working alongside each other. Also, this allows each person to take home his or her own project as a reminder of the day's lesson. On the other hand, a group project will help build a sense of community—especially helpful when the group as a whole is facing challenges—and create a finished product which can be displayed in a public place. Take into consideration the nature of the subject and the closeness of the relationships within the group to decide on this issue.

Driving myself to distraction

When an art project is thrust upon an unsuspecting group, you are dealing with many different levels of skill and experience in one room, and some people just may not be in touch with their creative side or feel free to explore it. If the creative process is about focusing on God, we may be less able to do that when others are watching our work, especially if art isn't our "thing." We are social creatures and cannot be with others without being aware of their presence and their interpretation of the choices we make (whether it be the shoes we're wearing or the lines we're painting). You may want to start small and work up to some of the experiments.

> "Just dash something down if you see a blank canvas staring at you with a certain imbecility. You do not know how paralysing it is, that staring of a blank canvas which says to the painter; You don't know anything. Many painters are afraid of the blank canvas, but the blank canvas is afraid of the real passionate painter who dares."
>
> —Vincent van Gogh, from *Dear Theo: The Autobiography of Vincent van Gogh*, edited by Irving Stone

The cool factor

There can be that sense in experimental worship experiences where we all understand how very postmodern and edgy we are—how very unlike our stuffy parents who worship in those traditional ways. Once more, this switches the focus from God to ourselves and ruins whatever atmosphere there could have been.

All this is not to say that it is impossible to use these experiments in group settings (in fact, we may be *more* able to lose ourselves and focus on God when we're not alone). However, using them in a group requires thought and sensitivity—careful consideration of the makeup of the group involved, the appropriateness of the project, and the way it will be introduced to the group.

Elements of Making and Meeting

BEING OK WITH FUN

"Go, eat your food with gladness, and drink your wine with a joyful heart, for it is now that God favors what you do."
—ECCLESIASTES 9:7

Christians have, throughout the ages, done some pretty weird things in the name of piety. In their efforts to put to death the flesh, believers in various times and places have worn purposefully irritating metal-spiked or prickly clothing, whipped themselves, bricked themselves into the walls of churches, and starved themselves of food, water, and human contact. A rather extreme example is Simeon Stylites, a third-century saint who, after realizing the difficulty of remaining pure in normal society, went through extreme deprivation in an effort to grow closer to God. When starving himself almost to death and living chained to a rock atop a mountain didn't have the effect he desired, he built himself a pillar (hence the name Stylites, which means pillar) and lived his remaining thirty-seven years perched on top of it. To occupy himself up there, he created strange and cruel duties to perform, including bowing to pray 1,200 times in a day and standing for two weeks without rest (Paul Burns, *Butler's Lives of the Saints*).

While we may snicker at such stories, our faith often still retains remnants of those earlier ways. Fun, for many faithful people, is, at best, a thing for kids and, at worst, an evil, worldly, or distracting thing. I suspect that much of the problem with fun for Christians is that it involves reveling in our senses, and that worries us. We're concerned that we might enjoy all this sensory stimulation so much that it will lead us away from God.

Do we see God as some kind of twisted creator who gave us the ability to see and touch and smell and taste the world around us in order to tempt us? Why not, instead, see him as a **generous creator** who, through our senses, **infuses our lives with color and texture and richness**? Strangely enough, we avoid the good things God has created because we're worried they'll lead us away from him; then we end up led away from him because we have deprived ourselves of true joy. I'm not talking about a religion of hedonism here—Paul warns us about being lovers of pleasure rather than lovers of God (2 Timothy 3:4). But couldn't we at least be *likers* of pleasure?

"The two experiences [of looking at paintings and sensing God through the reading of Scripture] are more similar than you might suppose. Not just because the experience of reading a book can be tactile or olfactory, but because the very subject matter of Scripture—human contact with the Divine—makes irresistible demands upon each of our senses if we are to understand anything at all about God."

—Roger Ferlo, *Sensing God*

King Solomon, in Ecclesiastes, struggles with the question of how much trust to put in worldly pleasures such as accomplishments, relationships, and possessions and, after much experimentation and pondering, he realizes none of them can satisfy. But his conclusion isn't to discard them altogether. Instead, he tells us simply to see them for what they are—good, but limited, **gifts from a good, and unlimited, God** (this concept is discussed more fully in my first book, *Life Is Too Important to Be Taken Seriously: Kite-Flying Lessons from Ecclesiastes*):

Go, eat your food with gladness, and drink your wine with a joyful heart, for it is now that God favors what you do. Always be clothed in white, and always anoint your head with oil. Enjoy life with your wife, whom you love, all the days of this meaningless life that God has given you under the sun—all your meaningless days. For this is your lot in life and in your toilsome labor under the sun. Whatever your hand finds to do, do it with all your might, for in the grave, where you are going, there is neither working nor planning nor knowledge nor wisdom. (Ecclesiastes 9:7-10)

The entire Bible overflows with sensory metaphors. In 2 Corinthians 2:14-16, Paul gets our nostrils twitching with: "But thanks be to God, who always leads us in triumphal procession in Christ and through us spreads everywhere the fragrance of the knowledge of him. For we are to God the aroma of Christ among those who are being saved and those who are perishing. To the one we are the smell of death; to the other, the fragrance of life." Our mouths water when we read in the Psalms, "How sweet are your words to my taste, sweeter than honey to my mouth!" (119:103). When we read in Mark 5:30, "At once Jesus realized that power had gone out from him. He turned around in the crowd and asked, 'Who touched my clothes?'" we wonder how it felt for the woman to touch Jesus, and how it felt

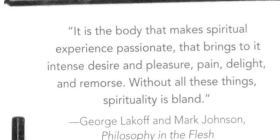

"It is the body that makes spiritual experience passionate, that brings to it intense desire and pleasure, pain, delight, and remorse. Without all these things, spirituality is bland."

—George Lakoff and Mark Johnson, *Philosophy in the Flesh*

There's a big tree in my backyard. I don't even know what kind it is, but it's a great climbing tree. Whenever I need a new perspective on life and the world, I climb it. It's probably no taller than my bedroom window, but for some reason the view from here is different. In the tree I feel closer to the creator of the trees. Ever since I learned that trees breathe out what we breathe in and we breathe out what they breathe in, I've seen them as partners and felt that God gave them to us as a gift. They provide us with carbon dioxide, wood, flowers, fruits, shade, and great places to climb.
—A. S.

RECIPE FOR A MESS

for Jesus to sense the healing power of God leave his body. Did it tickle? Our ears ring from John's description of a heavenly cacophony in Revelation 14:2, 3: "And I heard a sound from heaven like the roar of rushing waters and like a loud peal of thunder. The sound I heard was like that of harpists playing their harps. And **they sang a new song before the throne** and before the four living creatures and the elders." And, with Paul, our eyes strain to make out the features of a face when we read 1 Corinthians 13:12: "Now we see but a poor reflection as in a mirror; then we shall see face to face. Now I know in part; then I shall know fully, even as I am fully known."

How could we possibly hope to understand God if we ignored our senses? The authors of Scripture used these metaphors to **make a point** to people who had smelled death, tasted honey, and heard rushing waters. If we deny ourselves the richness of our senses, we deny ourselves the richness of the Bible. It opens with a lush garden, filled with delights and wonders, and ends with a magnificent city, filled with delights and wonders. Perhaps the mess and strife and evil in the pages and years between are caused not by the delights themselves, but by our misuse and fear of the **delights we have been given**.

TAKE A MOMENT

1. In 1 Corinthians 9:27, Paul says "I beat my body and make it my slave." How can we live out both the passage above from Ecclesiastes 9 and this one?

2. Can fun be a spiritual thing? How? What is fun for you? Can you involve God in it?

3. Can spirituality be a fun thing? How? What is spiritual for you? Can you make it fun?

Our Favorite Recipes

"Where can I go from your Spirit?
Where can I flee from your presence?"
—Psalm 139:7

The Themes: community, spirituality, God's presence
The Reading: Psalm 139

THE THINKING

What exactly is spirituality? When the team that plans our services saw this theme on the schedule, we were a little stumped. Isn't spirituality the theme every Sunday? How could we dedicate a whole service to it without doing the same things we always did? So we stopped to define what we thought spirituality really was and came to agree that it wasn't so much about being super-spiritual but about being aware of God's presence in our lives. We also agreed that this wasn't about going on some quest to find God but about remembering he is already here. We looked to Psalm 139 as our key passage, in which David expresses an intense awareness that God is in everything David does and is everywhere David is.

So our question then became: What would it look like to have that kind of appreciation for the fact that the creator of the universe takes part in every moment, every action of our lives? We knew immediately that the best place to look was in our own corner of the body of Christ, our own congregation, and how they lived their lives. We joked that churches usually put together recipe books, inviting each member to contribute their favorite recipes for cookies and casseroles. And we decided that instead we would invite our members to contribute their own, home-cooked recipes for spirituality. They gave me permission to share their ideas and practices, and so you'll see their "recipe cards" (all titled **Recipe for a Mess**) peppered throughout this book.

THE MAKING

Creating or, more likely, discovering these recipes can be as simple as thinking about your day or something you like to do, or habits you have. You may find them in words you read or stories you hear or bits of advice you listen to. The ones we collected came from things ordinary people did as a part of their ordinary lives as a way to get in touch with an extraordinary God. Here are a few examples of my church's recipes to give you a "taste."

> I love to walk on the beach—the sky and sea seem endless and remind me of how big God is. But I don't get to go to the beach very often, since it's many states away. Each time I do visit a beach, I collect stones and keep them in a bowl on my table. As I eat my meals each day, I see these stones from Canadian lakes and Scottish and American seas and remember the big skies of those beaches and the big God who is with me in my little house.
>
> —M. P.

It is in my house garden that I experience the Holy Spirit doing its work in me. He is a comforter. In the jungle of leaves, surrounded by the smell of good earth, I know that God is with me. The dirt that remains in my nails for days after reminds me that he is always constant . . . even if I am not.

—B. A.

I find something meaningful about the routine of preparation for the day. In Scripture we see that people prepared themselves by anointing, which brought a ritual of hygiene into a spiritual sphere. And so as I prepare for the day, it is natural to think and pray about what the day holds and who I will see. And when I'm done, I'm physically ready—hair's brushed, shoes are tied—but my heart, mind, and soul are ready too.

—A. S.

I have a habit of keeping little tokens in my pockets. In one coat I have an old map from a long hike and in a jacket I have a coin from a trip to Europe. In another pocket is a smooth stone my daughter gave me. Some of these coats may sit in the closet for months but as soon as I wear them again, and hide my hands in their pockets, I am reminded again of people and places, and how God was there with me and how he is with me now.

—A. P.

Whenever I hear an emergency vehicle siren, I say a little prayer for the person involved. Usually it means a house on fire or a car accident or someone in danger somehow, and I ask God to make his presence known to whoever is suffering at that moment.

—Anonymous

Choose one of these practices and adapt it for your life today or tomorrow, whether it's how you work, how you prepare for your day, planting mementos for yourself, finding prayer prompts in common sounds, or by simply appreciating God's creation. Try at least one and take note of how it affects your day.

MAKING IT WORK FOR SMALL GROUPS OR CORPORATE WORSHIP SETTINGS

One way to adapt this exercise for a group would be to collect some "recipes" ahead of time from various individuals and ask them if they would be willing to read them to the group. Have a corporate reading of Psalm 139:1-18, stopping every few verses to allow someone to share a recipe.

Or for a group or as part of a service, provide a large writing space. Paper rolls or whiteboards are great, but several pieces of poster board will work. Or be creative and use large, flat items from everyday life to help make the connection between worship and life (for example: an old door or mirror, a map, a flattened packing box). Be sure that the writing surfaces are clean and flat and blank enough that writing will be legible. Provide plenty of permanent markers and choose a working area large enough and/or in various places so that several people can write at once. Play reflective music or, during a worship music set, invite individuals to come and share their "recipes" through writing and/or drawing. Be sure to do this exercise after giving examples and a time of reflection so that people have had time to think and are ready to share.

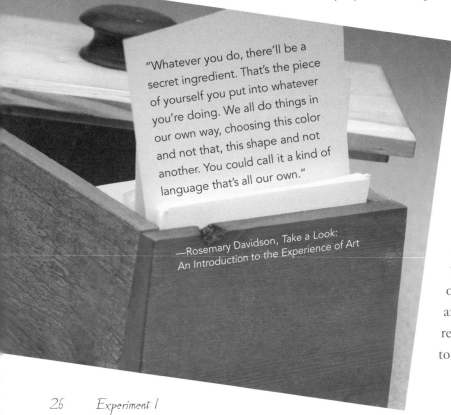

"Whatever you do, there'll be a secret ingredient. That's the piece of yourself you put into whatever you're doing. We all do things in our own way, choosing this color and not that, this shape and not another. You could call it a kind of language that's all our own."

—Rosemary Davidson, Take a Look: An Introduction to the Experience of Art

Compile the recipes in a blog, an online photo gallery, or a printed version to distribute to group members so that they may use each other's ideas.

THE MEETING

1. Read Psalm 139:1-18. What would this kind of awareness look like in your life?

2. In what other ways do you remind yourself that God is part of your life on a daily basis?

3. What recipes have you cooked up in your work, your household chores, your interaction with loved ones—when you drive and dress and shop and exercise? If you don't currently use these elements of life to remind you of God's presence, how could you begin to?

4. As you take part in a mundane routine, ask yourself: How can this become a way I remember God's part in my life? It may cause you to give thanks or to cry out for God's provision, to feel God's comfort or to call him to your side—in any case, you're involving God in what you're doing, thinking, and feeling, and so you're aware of his presence.

5. After you've tried out number 4 for a little while, come back here and ask yourself: How does this approach to routine practices change how I feel about my life? about God?

Where Is Your Victory?

*"When the perishable has been clothed with the imperishable, and the mortal with immortality,
then the saying that is written will come true: 'Death has been swallowed up in victory.'
'Where, O death, is your victory? Where, O death, is your sting?'"*

—1 CORINTHIANS 15:54, 55

The Themes: life, death, Jesus, resurrection, Easter, mortality, immortality, victory

The Reading: Matthew 27:57–28:7; 1 Corinthians 15:51–57

THE THINKING

To explain the connection between Easter and eggs, a children's book says "The eggs are eggstra." It's catchy and cute, but is it true? Of course, Easter is all **wrapped up** in fertility and spring festivals from ancient times, but perhaps our poet God planned for Jesus to rise from the dead in spring for a reason. Eggs are **tiny miracles**. What better way to remind us every year of the miracle of Easter? Every year, as we hang eggs on our little

German egg tree, I say to my kids: "Look, an egg doesn't look like much does it? In fact, it could be mistaken for a lifeless rock. But what's inside? Does that remind you of any other **lifeless rocks that were hiding life?**" This year I heard my older child explaining it to my younger—so I know it's slowly sinking in.

It's interesting how much a stone features in the Easter story. It's mentioned in all the Gospels' tellings of either the burial or resurrection, or both. We read in Matthew 27 that Joseph of Arimathea rolled a large stone across the entrance to Jesus' tomb and that Pilate's guards also sealed the stone. Both Joseph and the guards felt security in that rock. But by the next morning the strength of the rock is shown to be nothing in comparison to the **power of the life within it**.

Death seems like a rock—**solid** and indisputable. It will not be reasoned with or cajoled. It seems to have the final word, the victory. And yet, Jesus reveals it to be as delicate as eggshells. And so **we can boldly** look death in the eye and ask "Where is your victory? Where is your sting?"

THE MAKING

Gather the following materials:

- 1-2 rinsed and dried eggshells per person
- craft glue
- paintbrushes
- wooden board or heavy cardboard at least 6 inches square (Be sure that the board/cardboard is a color which will contrast the color of eggshells. If it's not, paint it.)
- paints, optional
- pencil
- glass or cup approximately 3 inches in diameter, for tracing around

Before this exercise, you'll need to empty the eggs (and make a nice omelet, if you like), rinse the shells, and allow them to dry. It is OK to crack the eggs, but try to keep the majority of the shell intact—more deliberate breaking will happen later.

If you like, paint the board to resemble a hillside. This can be as simple as drawing a curved line and painting it in with green. Allow the paint to dry.

Mark a circle approximately 3 inches in diameter in the center of the hill or board by tracing around a cup. This will represent the entrance to the tomb.

Slowly and carefully break off pieces of the eggshell(s) and position them to fill the circle, like a mosaic. Glue them in place as you go (it may be easier to brush glue onto the board in a small section than to paint it onto the eggshell). If you break off a piece of eggshell approximately a half inch across, you can press it down flat onto a glued area.

It will break as you press and the pieces will form a mosaic effect. Keep adding more pieces, choosing shapes which will fill the gaps and complete the circle.

As you place the pieces of broken eggshell, reflect on the fragility of the tomb where Jesus' body was laid. Allow the exercise to remind you of the day a huge boulder was revealed to be as invincible as eggshells.

MAKING IT WORK FOR SMALL GROUPS OR CORPORATE WORSHIP SETTINGS

Provide enough materials for people to do individual projects or to make a large project together. If doing a large project, think about what size the surface and the circle need to be to allow everyone a chance to work together. You could use a large piece of cardboard, plywood, or even an old door or table as your background. Just test the surface to see that it is flat and clean enough for the eggshell pieces to stick to it. Be sure to provide each person his own eggshell to break.

RECIPE FOR A MESS

When I'm stressed or worried or am just forgetting about joy, the sun reminds me of God. I feel the sun on my skin and I am reminded that God has given us another day and I have to smile. It is a reminder of how much God loves me.
—Anonymous

A group project may be helpful for a community during a time of grief, as a reminder that death does not have the victory. Or work a project like this into your group's Easter traditions. If you celebrate Lent, work on the group project over the forty days so that it is complete by Easter Sunday. You could set the project up in a hall or foyer, leave the glue and eggshells in a container near the background, and invite people to take a moment to break off some pieces and add to the mosaic as they pass by.

To make a group art piece to display during the Easter season, make a cross from two beams (making sure that the wood is flat and clean enough to paste the eggshell onto it) and draw circles along its length (in a pattern if you like). Be sure they're far enough apart to allow each individual to work on her own eggshell circle. Provide the eggshells and glue and give the group time to complete their circles. This project may communicate that the cross had resurrection built into it.

This piecing together of eggshells takes on the effect of puzzle making. Since the mysteries of Christ's death and resurrection are puzzling and take some time to piece together, a puzzle is a fitting Easter metaphor. Purchase a large jigsaw puzzle of Christ on the cross or some other part of the Easter story. (Ricordi Arte makes beautiful puzzles of the artworks *Christ of St. John of the Cross* and *Christo Morto* which are available online.) We have a thousand-piece puzzle of the crucifixion which we leave out in our church/café the week leading up to Easter so that our church and wider community can, over time, piece it together.

"But chiefly we are bound to praise thee for the glorious Resurrection of thy Son Jesus Christ our Lord: for he is the very Paschal Lamb, which was offered for us, and hath taken away the sin of the world; who by his death hath destroyed death, and by his rising to life again hath restored to us everlasting life."

—The Easter Communion Reading from *The Book of Common Prayer*

THE MEETING

1. In what ways does life seem fragile to you? When you consider your own health or the failing health of a loved one? Or your inability to find the meaning in it all?

2. What kind of feelings do you have when you think about death? As you were making a tomb out of eggshells, how did that impact your thinking about death? about the hope and victory we have in Jesus?

3. Did you see the Easter story in a different way? How is death fragile because of Easter?

4. How much do you feel death has been defeated in our world? How often do you feel like death still has its victories? Why?

TAKING IT TO THE STREET

In the weeks leading up to Easter, send out a group to hang real, blown-out eggs in the trees lining local streets or in a local park, or on your church's property. (Go online to learn how to blow the eggs.) Local people will wonder what it all means. Add some signs if you want to use it as an opportunity to ask questions about the point of Easter or to promote your Easter services. Ask your group to take note of how long the eggs last. Leave the eggs their natural color and use natural twine so that they biodegrade.

Elements of Making and Meeting

LEARNING TO ENJOY THE PROCESS

*"Make it your ambition to lead a quiet life, to mind your own business
and to work with your hands, just as we told you."*
—1 Thessalonians 4:11

Two days ago I flew across the world. Well, my body did. I seem to have left my brain (and my good mood) somewhere on the other side of the Pacific. And so, devoid of sound mind and pleasant mood, I have before me five weeks of mail to sort and bills to pay, five weeks of clothes to unpack and launder, five weeks of photos to download and print, and, most overwhelming of all, five weeks of experiences and conversations to process. While I have these mounting chores, the only thing I really, really, really want to do—and the only thing I can't do—is sleep. So, I groggily face the bills and the suitcases.

I've decided that human beings aren't designed to zoom across planets at 500 miles per hour. We're not supposed to go from winter in the tropics to summer in the coniferous zone in a matter of hours. Seasons change over the course of months, and yet last Friday I breakfasted in wintry Australia and lunched in balmy USA.

We've heard that jet lag is all about the tilt and rotation of the planet and the international dateline, but I think it's more than that. Flying 10,000 miles in 23 hours (or, for that matter, driving 600 miles in 9 hours) moves our bodies through space. But can our minds (and spirits) keep up? Can they fathom what it means to be leaving where we're leaving and arriving where we're arriving in the brief time it takes to physically leave and arrive? In the days when we relied on human and animal legs for transport, our insides had time to keep up. Perhaps, to the usual list of factors contributing to our generation's record levels of stress and depression, we should add our regular habit of hurtling through space at 65 (or more) miles per hour.

These are my ponderings as I begrudgingly tackle my chores. And yet, as I embrace the tedium of sorting and cleaning, I discover that I'm sorting more than my mail and cleaning more than my clothes. My mind and spirit are catching up with my new location and somehow, by going through the process, *I'm* able to process.

In how many other ways do we skip the noun *process* and miss the verb *process*? More than just a temporary jet lag, do we live in an ongoing life lag? When we buy our carrots pre-peeled, kill our weeds chemically, call our friends on autodial, buy our food/clothes/furnishings ready-made, do we skip a step? Could the simple acts of peeling carrots, pulling weeds, writing letters, knitting, kneading, sanding, or painting have some value?

The Jetsons lived life at the push of a button and seemed so well adjusted, but I'd like to know: if she never swept, when did Jane Jetson figure out how to deal with her boy-crazy teenager; and if he never walked, when did George ever weigh up the options and decide that Spacely Sprockets was the right career move? While we're not quite the Jetsons, we have become too accustomed to the conveniences of modern life to do away entirely with all the shortcuts. But occasionally, taking the long way might find us happier.

As a little luxury, choose the long way to clean or cook or travel or communicate and see if it finds you praying, reflecting, or understanding more. You may find it tedious, or, by some miracle, you may find yourself where you are when you're there.

> "The modern world lays such emphasis on the work *product* and stresses productivity so relentlessly that process is only seen as a means to this end. . . . Process is, I would like to stress, one of those words we cannot slight when we speak of art—or growth, for that matter. The healing properties of the experience are bound into the process."
> —Joan M. Erikson, *Wisdom and the Senses: The Way of Creativity*

TAKE A MOMENT

1. Do you ever feel like you're just keeping up with life? How often do you feel mentally, emotionally, or spiritually unprepared for the tasks of your day?

2. What are one or two slow activities you could add to your day? Think about something you normally use a shortcut for—could you do it the long way every now and then to allow your mind and spirit time to catch up?

3. What kinds of chores do you do with a noisy piece of equipment? Think about getting rid of the noise a few times a week and instead, turning that chore into an opportunity for your hands (and spirit) to work in quietness.

4. Try adding some of the following to your routine:

    walking or bicycling   sweeping manually

    polishing woodwork   making or fixing something with your hands

    cooking from scratch

While it may mean getting the job done or going somewhere more slowly, resist the urge to rush it. Rushing switches your mind into a stress mode, which is never a good mode for prayer or reflection. You may find that, although you took more time to complete the task, you are more productive when you get back to the "important" things because your mind and spirit are ready and refreshed.

RECIPE FOR A MESS

When I was a seminary student, I read a lot of things about prayer, including discussions of the right time, right place, right posture, right props. But I was the parent of two toddlers, working half-time, attending school full-time, and trying to learn how to be an adult. I then read the medieval author Thomas à Kempis, who described the "prayer of rumination." Rumination means, literally, chewing your cud: turning things over in your mind and heart as you go about your day, like Mary, who quietly "pondered these things in her heart." Rumination is conducting a constant inward conversation with God in which my heart is open to him to "read" and "hear," and I try to learn to read and hear his heart. I realized then that there is no right place, right time, or right technique for sinners with dirty hands who live in the stream of history, family, work, and commitment. I realized that my best prayer happened, in fact, while I washed the dishes in the evening. I valued that time. I valued focusing, like Martha, on the work of my hands, as a way of opening myself to Christ: not the "better part," but the only part I had to give at that stage of my life.

I still love to wash the dishes, though I also like having teenagers who can help! When I wash, I'm able to turn my attention inward, examine my conscience, offer repentance and praise to God, open my heart to him and pour it out, and finally keep quiet so that I can hear what he might say about how, in me, his kingdom can come and his will be done, here on earth, just as it is in his heaven.

—P. N.

Beauty in Brokenness

"Behold, I am making all things new."
—REVELATION 21:5 (*NASB*)

The Themes: redemption, resurrection, hope, suffering, endurance, perseverance, beauty
The Reading: Revelation 21:1-5

THE THINKING

When a friend asked me to create something to hang on the walls of his counseling center, I wanted to make something hopeful, but not sugary sweet, honest, but not cynical. It had to acknowledge both brokenness and healing. The kids who visited the center would see right through any attempts to gloss over the challenges of life and certainly didn't need any more darkness than they already had.

Each of us **experiences the brokenness of the world** in different ways. For some it feels internal; for them the human condition is very personal. They feel incurably flawed. For others, the oppression comes from the **brokenness of the external world**—life has handed them a complex mess. Whether we experience the brokenness by being the victim of crime or of a manipulative parent, by feeling physical or emotional pain, by wishing for something that can never be or regretting something that was, our lives are far from the perfect things we would like them to be. But God's triumphant words in Revelation promise he'll **make it all right again**.

This project may function as a reminder that your own imperfection can be used by God for good or perhaps may work to encourage you that **you can create** something good from the less-than-perfect situation you have been handed.

THE MAKING

This art project is a kind of motley mosaic. To prepare, begin collecting broken, useless, ugly things. It may take days or weeks to collect enough, but over the course of that time, you'll find a new appreciation for objects you'd otherwise see as pointless. I'm sure my neighbors were puzzled by my new interest in the rusty bolts in the middle of the street and the Christmas lights in their trash. I had most luck under beds, in junk drawers (wherever spare change, rubber bands, and old keys collect), and, of course, in the trash can. And I didn't feel it was cheating to buy a few chipped plates from Goodwill too, because someone obviously had decided they weren't of value. (And smashing them was quite therapeutic, although I would suggest you put them in a large paper sack before the smashing begins. It's much easier to pick up the bits.)

Find an old wooden board or background which is sturdy enough to hold heavy objects (a stretched canvas may not hold up but a canvas board may). The board doesn't have to be new or clean—in fact, it may add to the effect of the finished work if you find something also seen as useless (an old bulletin board or stained cutting board, perhaps?). Alternatively, find an old photo frame, remove the card or wood backing, and glue the glass to the frame. This will make a mini-window to use as your background.

You'll also need some serious glue: one that dries clear, that doesn't expand too much, and doesn't need much clamping, if possible. Look for one that will stick to many different surfaces, since it's likely you'll be working with plastic, wood, paper, metal, glass, etc. You may find that superglue or a glue gun works for you. I found a great glue, grandly named Omni-Stick, made by Hammerhead (although it could have also been called "Omni-*Stink*"). Things will stick more easily if they're clean, so give anything greasy or dirty a wipe (without wiping away its sadness, if possible).

You may want to outline a shape first. For my three works, I chose simple images, all alluding to nature—one, a sun-like image, with beams radiating from a round center; another, a simplified wave; and a third, a curling leaf shoot (as shown on pages 38 and 40). You may want to choose a simple face, tree, leaf, shell, or geometric shape. Is there a shape that is meaningful to you?

Sort your collected items into colors to function as your palette. Then begin arranging them on your backing board, filling in the shapes you've sketched with groups of same-colored items until you're happy with the result (this is like coloring, but instead of filling a shape with crayon, you're filling it with a collection of small items that are the same color). Don't feel you have to either fill the entire space or stop at the edge of the board—I allowed pieces of glass to extend past the edges of the board to add a

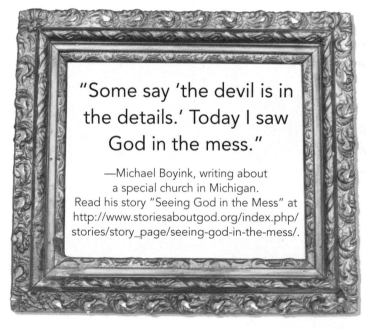

"Some say 'the devil is in the details.' Today I saw God in the mess."

—Michael Boyink, writing about a special church in Michigan. Read his story "Seeing God in the Mess" at http://www.storiesaboutgod.org/index.php/stories/story_page/seeing-god-in-the-mess/.

sense of movement to the work. Stand back and admire. You may find that it comes together as one piece when you're farther from it. Now the gluing can begin. Allow ample time for your work to dry. Then carefully hang or display your finished piece wherever you desire.

Making it work for small groups or corporate worship settings

Over the course of several weeks or studies (especially if you're covering topics like perseverance/renewal), **ASK MEMBERS TO COLLECT** discarded/broken objects. Stipulate that each object should be small enough to fit in the palm of their hands, not gross, and fairly clean. If you'd like, you can also suggest a particular color. The collection process is as important as the creation process, so don't rush it. If you're on a retreat, **PROVIDE FREE TIME** for participants to go for a walk and raid the trash.

INVITE THE GROUP to choose a shape to create together. Set a time for them to bring their collected items and provide labeled boxes so that items can be sorted by color. Provide a large background board with the agreed-upon shape already penciled in and marked with where each color should go (think of it as paint-by-numbers except you're filling each space with pieces of colored glass/wood/metal/plastic instead of paint). Invite the group to arrange the pieces on the board (it's OK not to use every piece of junk) to **CREATE THE DESIRED SHAPE** and then have everyone step back to admire the overall effect. Doing this project as a group will incorporate a sense of community, which may be helpful if there is a need for hope or healing. Display the piece in a public place within your church or community to **ALLOW PEOPLE TO CONTINUE TO REFLECT** on the project.

However, if you'd prefer that **GROUP MEMBERS FOCUS** on individual hope or healing, provide small pieces of backing board and allow them to choose their own shapes and arrangements of junk. This will allow individuals to take and keep their own pieces as a reminder of this lesson.

THE MEETING

/. When you were collecting the junk to use in your collage, did it make you see things in a new way? If so, how?

2. Notice how the broken pieces came together to create something new. How do they look up close? How do they look when you are standing farther away?

3. How do the pieces of your life look up close? How do they look when you stand back and try to see them as a whole?

4. List the things that you would consider broken in your life or world. In what ways can you find new hope, new meaning, or new opportunities in those less-than-ideal things?

TAKING IT TO THE STREET

In 2007 the city of Cincinnati took part in this art experiment that we called The Collect—which was a play on the word *collect* since, in addition to the obvious meaning, the Collect (pronounced with the emphasis on the first syllable) is a section of traditional Christian liturgy, used to call the congregation to worship together. Through local media I invited members of the public to bring their junk to any of six cafés. Over the course of a month, the boxes filled up with old glasses and keys, camera parts and toys, at which point I turned them over to seventeen artists, who spent a few months transforming them into works of art. Finally, we had a month-long coffee shop art show to display the wonders which had been worked from trash, and auctioned all the art to benefit an inner-city youth art project. This was a great way to

RECIPE FOR A MESS

I've journaled for some time and it was helpful to a degree, but recently I adapted the traditional practice and it means so much more to me. My journal before was writing how I felt about things but I often felt I had to have my ideas all worked out before I wrote them down. So I didn't write very often. But now I use my journal as a place to collect the raw materials of my thoughts, instead of the finished product. So now it holds sketches, newspaper clippings, prayers, Bible passages, photos, mementos. Once I've collected all these little scraps from my life, I can see the themes running through them and understand the lessons God is teaching me.

—M. L. M.

reach out to the community, to make something together, to clean up the streets, raise money for a local charity, and just have fun.

See how you can adapt the project for your community. Instead of coffee shops, schools, libraries, or churches could function as drop-off or art show locations. Instead of auctioning individual pieces for charity, could the artist(s) make a sculpture to exhibit in a public place? Or, instead of large artworks, could they create small, affordable pieces such as jewelry?

Many artists work with "found objects" (what used to be called junk) and come up with some amazing things. The British duo, Tim Noble and Sue Webster, create piles of garbage which seem random and ugly and yet, when lit, their shadows create wonderful shapes and images—another example of meaning found in seeming meaninglessness. Search online for "real life is rubbish" images by Noble and Webster.

This piece of art titled *Price Hill Easter* appeared in The Collect, 2007.

> *"He has showed you, O man, what is good.*
> *And what does the Lord require of you?*
> *To act justly and to love mercy and to*
> *walk humbly with your God."*
> —MICAH 6:8

EXPERIMENT
4

Walk Humbly

The Themes: faith, humility, perseverance, beauty, life, obedience
The Reading: Micah 6:1-8

THE THINKING

"Act justly" and "love mercy" seem straightforward enough. But what is it to "walk humbly"? Is it to doubt your own strength? To bumble along, mumbling about your own inadequacies?

On a nasty, nasty afternoon I set out to pick up my two children plus the two who ride with us. If I ever doubt my maternal instincts, that obstacle course with four small dawdlers—from the school to the car every afternoon, past noisy school buses and over busy streets—reminds me I'm a red-blooded mother. But this day I felt an extra ruffle in my maternal feathers, and it wasn't just the high wind. The closest parking spot left me a long, cold march from the school and I dreaded, in my umbrella-less state, the prospect of a wet and windy walk with four drippy kids.

It didn't help that I just wanted to be home in my pajamas. I was having a low week and longed to be safe and warm. So as I leaned into the wind and squinted against the rain, my inaudible wail to God was, *I know life is*

*hard. I don't expect you to protect me from everything. But sometimes it would be nice. **Sometimes I need that kind of love that bundles me up and says, "I'll make it better."** If I long to provide that for four weary school children, don't you sometimes long to do that for me?*

With my chin tucked in against the rain, there was little else to do but watch the rhythmic plod of my feet. They just kept moving. My weary mind marveled at those unstoppable feet. As much as my head wanted to be home and warm, my legs somehow kept slicing through the icy air. In their sensible shoes, my feet were oblivious to my fragile mental state. They didn't just plant themselves and pout. They didn't admit defeat and go home. No, somehow, those feet kept me walking. Well, of course I walked because I had children to pick up and what kind of adult would say "I couldn't pick up the kids today because it was too drizzly." It really wasn't an option, but you know what I mean.

Life is hard and cold and windy and we'd like God to just make it all better (and sometimes he does but rarely as much as, or when, we'd like). And yet life has a way of continuing. **We're stronger than we think.** Our feet keep moving, in spite of the fact that our mouths are saying "I can't do this."

So for me, walking humbly means just walking. And walking. And walking some more. Even when you don't know why you walk or where you walk. Even when you just want to go home. To walk humbly is to trust there's a point, to bite your tongue when you want to demand an explanation from God, to grasp desperately onto the possibility that he knows what he's doing.

> **To walk humbly is to**
> **wonder where you're going.**
> **And walk anyway.**

THE MAKING

Gather the following materials:

- wooden board, at least a foot or two long and wide, but as big as you like (I chose a long, narrow board because it reminded me of a floorboard. It doesn't have to be new; in fact, it may be more interesting if it's something you found in the back shed. Dirt or oil will prevent paint from sticking, though, so watch out for that).
- acrylic paints
- fine-point permanent marker
- clean, bare feet
- lots of rags/paper towels/old towels and a bathtub or large bucket of soapy water
- drop cloth

A detail from a foot-painted board, like the one shown on page 44.

Cover the floor with your drop cloth and lay your board on it. Be sure your rags and water are close by. Choose two or more colors of paint and squirt it at random intervals onto the board.

Now comes the fun part. Remove your shoes and socks and walk back and forth through the paint. Paint is surprisingly slippery, so you might want to have a chair or friend nearby to hold onto (although, the metaphor of the imprint of a rear end might be poignant!). Try not to dictate where the colors go—just cover the board with footprints. Does life sometimes feel as messy and random as this? As nonsensical and squelchy?

When you feel you've stomped around enough, go and have a good scrub. Now let the paint dry. And take some time to look at the mess. Leave your painted board where you'll see it regularly so you can explore it each day.

RECIPE FOR A MESS

When I run, he

runs with me.

—Anonymous

It might take a while to find them but can you see patterns and shapes that make sense? a curled leaf or a row of birds sitting on a fence? a perfect circle or the letter *P*? Just as it takes time to find meaning and goodness in the mess of life, it might take several visits to your footwork to find something of beauty. It took me around fifteen minutes to do the foot painting part and about two weeks to find the shapes—an owl here, half a face there.

Now, take your fine-point marker (ideally in a color that contrasts the existing painting). Sit quietly and carefully outline the meaning in the mess. If you find twenty points of meaning/interest, outline them all. Or focus on one pattern or image that is especially meaningful or beautiful.

Living life can be an ongoing stumble of stubby toes, but finding beauty, purpose, and God in it takes careful study and a fine point.

RECIPE FOR A MESS

When I paint, I am humbled by the creative process. And I connect with my Creator God who made the colors and lines and textures and light.
—M. M.

MAKING IT WORK FOR SMALL GROUPS OR CORPORATE WORSHIP SETTINGS

Bear in mind the mess factor when planning this for a group activity. Can it be done outside or in a space that is easy to clean? Be sure to provide plenty of water and rags for cleanup. Consider if people will feel comfortable removing their shoes. Another (less messy) option is to provide markers and ask individuals to **COVER THE BOARD** with outlines of their feet. As these shapes overlap, they will still create recognizable patterns and shapes which can be outlined or filled in with a marker of a **CONTRASTING COLOR**.

Decide if you'd like this to be an individual activity which is done in a group or an activity the group does together. Will they create one final product for the group or one for each participant? If you'd like it to be a group activity, provide one large board for the **GROUP TO CREATE TOGETHER**. Be prepared for some giggling and hijinks. When the board is dry, place it in a public place and provide fine-point permanent markers so that, as people pass, they can search for patterns and meaning in the mess and sketch them in.

To create an individual activity, provide smaller boards. If you'd like it to remain entirely personal, allow them to take the boards home to outline points of meaning themselves. Or it may be powerful to allow the group to outline pieces of meaning in each other's (this may communicate that our community can help us make sense of the mess of our lives).

THE MEETING

Study your completed artwork.

1. What elements are you happy with? What would you change? Why?

2. How did you feel when walking through the paint?

3. Study the images/patterns you found in the footprints. How do they make you feel? Which one is your favorite and why?

4. How can you apply these lessons to your walk with God? Are there ways in which God seems to be asking you to walk without knowing where you're going?

5. How can you walk humbly? Is there meaning or beauty in the parts of your life which seem to be only messy and confusing?w

In his heart a man plans his course, but the Lord determines his steps.
—Proverbs 16:9

Elements of Making and Meeting

THE POWER OF RITUAL

"Do this in remembrance of me."
—LUKE 22:19

Last Tuesday, my grandfather followed me everywhere I went. At a store, flannel shirts reminded me of him. At home, the smell of steeping tea took me to his kitchen. It wasn't until late that night that I realized the date and it all made sense to me. It was the anniversary of his death. My neck knew that it was wearing the same scarf and my forehead felt the same November mist that it had felt on that same day, eight years ago. My forehead and my neck knew "He died today," long before my brain worked it out.

For many who are from an evangelical tradition, ritual is not a good thing. It often is paired with *mindless* or is made synonymous with *rut*. We are afraid that if we do the same religious activity each day or week we'll lose the real meaning behind it or turn into worship zombies. On the other hand, we have no problem with the word *tradition*. In many ways, they are the same. It wouldn't feel like Christmas without the tree, perhaps only partly because of the way the tree *looks*. Perhaps it also feels like Christmas because our hands associate the carrying of boxes from the attic and the untangling of lights with Christmas. We have done what we do each year to make it Christmas and so, it is Christmas.

We all know that there's a two-way communication between our brains and our bodies. We understand that the inner self communicates to the outer self—our brains sense dehydration, so orient our bodies toward a source of water. We also understand that the way we perceive the outer self affects the inner self—if we are self-conscious about a physical attribute, it will affect our moods, decisions, and values. And of course, we learn about the world around us through the body's five senses—our skin tells us when the sun is out; our noses tell us dinner's almost ready. But we don't give a lot of attention to how much the inner self learns from outer movements and actions—how our outer postures affect our inner postures. Recent research has come up with some almost unbelievable findings which *blur the boundaries* of our "emotional" and "physical" categories.

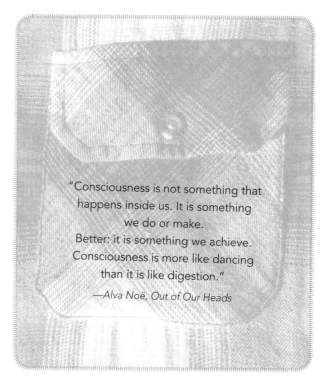

"Consciousness is not something that happens inside us. It is something we do or make.
Better: it is something we achieve. Consciousness is more like dancing than it is like digestion."

—Alva Noë, *Out of Our Heads*

In one study, when subjects were asked "to mimic either the long 'e' sound in 'cheese' (which required them to smile) or the German 'für' (which required them to pucker their lips, mimicking a negative emotional expression)," they tended to feel the emotion that their faces were inadvertently expressing. In other words, perhaps you're happy *because* you're smiling (Elaine Hatfield, John T. Cacioppo, and Richard L. Rapson, *Emotional Contagion*). *Try smiling now*—did you notice a slight lightening of your spirits?

Another study found that, when participants were asked to either nod or shake their heads (supposedly to test headphones they were wearing) while listening to certain messages, those asked to nod reported a more positive response to the message than those who were asked to shake their heads (Pablo Briñol and Richard E. Petty, "Overt Head Movements and Persuasion: A Self-Evaluation Analysis," *Journal of Personality and Social Psychology*).

Perhaps *our bodies communicate to our minds and souls* in ways we never knew! And perhaps God knew this about us long before psychologists discovered it. After all, he's the one who instituted many rituals and

RECIPE FOR A MESS

In our house, tea is an important ritual. We start the day with it, and it's the first thing we offer guests. An unstated part of the tea-making is the fact that it is poured from one large pot and we each hold a cup of it and so, in many ways, it's like communion—a daily reminder that we're all from the same source.

—Anonymous

traditions of the Judeo-Christian faith, including Sabbath-keeping, sacrifices, baptism, and Communion. If we taste a little juice every Sunday while contemplating Jesus' sacrifice, we will find ourselves in that frame of mind as soon as we pick up that little cup. How can this also be true outside of the church service? If we pray every night in the shower, we will find ourselves in an attitude of prayer as soon as we turn on the faucet. If we reflect on our favorite psalm every time we drive, the feel of the steering wheel will bring that psalm to mind. We're not so different from Pavlov's dogs. They salivated by association. We can worship by association.

 TAKE **A** MOMENT

1. What traditions are meaningful in your life and the lives of the people you live or have relationships with? Consider the big, annual traditions but also the small daily or weekly ones. Take a moment here to describe them and what they mean to you, how they contribute to your life and the lives of those involved.

2. How do your traditions build the group that you're a part of, whether that group is your family, team, neighborhood, or church?

3. What sensory experiences are involved in the traditions you mentioned? What kinds of physical movements? How are they part of the meaning of your traditions?

4. What traditions could you create to build relationships within your family or church or between yourself and God?

> *"I know that everything God does will endure forever; nothing can be added to it and nothing taken from it."*
> —Ecclesiastes 3:14

EXPERIMENT
5

Practicing Perfection

The Themes: imperfection, perfection, playfulness, faith, freedom, brokenness, contentment, control

The Reading: Ecclesiastes 1:15; 3:9-14

THE THINKING

Alexander Overwijk is my hero. Somehow I came across a YouTube video of him doing his thing and instantly this relative unknown won a place among Van Gogh and Bach in my eyes. Alexander Overwijk is the World Freehand Circle Drawing Champion. Not only did watching him create a beautiful circle make me marvel at his skill, I longed for that perfection and had to know how to do it myself.

I have to confess: I'm a recovering perfectionist. And so is my seven-year-old. As a toddler, Kieran didn't like his sandwiches cut because that meant they were broken. Bananas were a precarious snack because of their tendency to break in two. My husband and I often retell the story of the day we gave him a cookie with the letter *K* on it. He took one look and pointed out that one of the lines was crooked. In an effort to help him be OK with imperfection, I gave him a choice: "Well, there aren't any other cookies. You can eat that or put it in the trash." To our amazement, he very matter-of-factly popped it in the trash and WENT TO PLAY.

I reminded Kieran of this story at the breakfast table today. Now that he's bigger, he can laugh about it. After reminiscing about his dislike of cut sandwiches I asked, "You liked whole pieces of bread. But how did I get the pieces of bread?" Of course, he knows now that they had been cut from a loaf. And what did they have to do to the wheat to make the flour? And what had to happen to the wheat plant to harvest the grain? And what had to happen to the seed to grow the wheat? Brokenness is a part of everything, sometimes a necessary part.

"He sits enthroned above the Circle of the earth." —Isaiah 40:22

At moments in life, we each feel the reality of the sentiment in Ecclesiastes 1:15: **"What is twisted cannot be straightened; what is lacking cannot be counted."** And we feel very strongly that, as Solomon adds in chapter 3 "God has set eternity in the hearts of men." We can understand perfection and get tiny hints of a previous perfect state but it's out of our reach. Somehow nature is able to create perfect circles effortlessly, in bubbles, in eyes—we even live on a beautifully round sphere. When, in the fourteenth century, the Pope asked artist Giotto di Bondone to send a painting to prove his skill, Bondone simply drew a perfect circle. Like us, he knew that, while nature performs this miracle daily, there are few things more difficult for a human than to create a seemingly simple circle.

After declaring that God has set eternity—**a taste for goodness and perfection**—in the hearts of men, Solomon adds, "Yet they cannot fathom what God has done from beginning to end. I know that there is nothing better for men than to be happy and do good while they live. That everyone may eat and drink, and find satisfaction in all his toil—this is the gift of God. I know that everything God does will endure forever; nothing can be added to it and nothing taken from it" (Ecclesiastes 3:11-14).

Solomon acknowledges that we can't have the perfection that we long for, and yet he is OK with that. He describes a life of peace, of getting on with things and enjoying daily blessings, and finishes with a reminder of how we can do this: by letting God be God.

Gather materials for this simple experiment:

- large whiteboard or chalkboard or large sheets of paper (such as a paper roll)
- markers/chalk

Preparation

Set up the whiteboard/chalkboard/sheets of paper so that they are against a wall or at least vertical and sturdy. Make sure the surfaces start around hip-height of the people who will be drawing and extend as high as a foot over their heads.

Watch the online videos of Alexander Overwijk and the World Freehand Circle Drawing Championship Ottawa 2007 (search for those words on www.youtube.com). You'll see in the championship video that several children are involved, so it's not a terribly difficult skill. Standing beside a large board, the contestants keep their elbows still and use their forearms like a compass. (You can also search for video of the artist Tom Marioni drawing a larger freehand circle by swinging his entire arm, keeping his shoulder as the center of the circle.) While it takes some time to perfect the skill of making a circle, I was surprised how easy it is to make something that looks very much like a circle.

RECIPE FOR A MESS

I often worried if I was getting closer or farther away from God. Each new transgression, I believed, took me far away. Until. Until I thought of our relationship as one attached by a string. Each time I faltered, the string would snap. Every knot to restore the connection only brought us closer. Now I don't worry so much . . . I have more time to say "Thank you, God, for your amazing grace!"

—T. K. D.

After watching the video footage, limber up and give it a go. Like life, sometimes the less you think about it and the more flamboyance you show, the better the result. Stand back and look at your circle. Draw another. You'll find that if you keep drawing in the same place,

eventually, the effect of fifteen or twenty less-than-perfect circles will produce one not-quite-perfect but very nice circle.

Gather these materials for a more complex experiment:

- a large (at least four-foot square) piece of clear glass (An old window or glass door would be great—just be sure to clean and dry it.)
- permanent markers
- a large box of crayons (You don't need to buy a new box—this is a great way to recycle the broken stubs from school or church. You'll need to peel the paper labels off.)
- kitchen grater or vegetable peeler
- hair dryer
- rulers

Choose a selection of crayons within a color range (for example, different shades of blue). Lie the piece of glass flat and begin grating or peeling the crayons onto it. Moving as you go, and using the rulers to cover sections of glass or to scrape the flakes of crayon, make a square or rectangle of crayon shavings. Cover the area well—it will take four to five crayons to make an eight-inch square.

Using the hair dryer, blow hot air on the underside of the glass to melt the crayon shavings (being sure not to turn on the dryer unless it is under the glass, or the shavings will fly everywhere). After a minute or two, you will see the shavings become glossy and begin to spread. Watch how the colors blend and patterns form in the melted wax. Enjoy what is happening without needing to control it. Try to keep the general shape of the rectangle or square. Is this difficult?

Moving the hair dryer slowly, melt all the crayon shavings. If necessary, add more shavings or slowly tilt the glass to let the wax slide around the glass and then lie the glass flat. Allow this shape to cool and set while you begin shaving more crayons for more shapes.

When I did this exercise, I chose to make a quilt-like patchwork with six rectangles of melted crayons, because a patchwork is about making something from scraps, being OK with less-than-perfect circumstances.

When the crayon shapes are done and set, flip the glass to the other side and set it up against a wall so that it is sturdy and at a height that works for drawing freehand circles. It should be as close to perpendicular to the floor as possible. Take your permanent marker and practice your circles, one over the other.

MAKING IT WORK FOR SMALL GROUPS OR CORPORATE WORSHIP SETTINGS

Since the freehand circle drawing method described above takes a little practice, and a group setting may not allow time or space for it, just give the group a few minutes to try drawing a perfect circle in the usual way, on a small piece of paper. This will still create both yearning for perfection and frustration with imperfection. Or,

Seventeenth-century German mathematician Johannes Kepler saw, in the wholeness and perfection of the sphere, an image of God (see Jamie James, *The Music of the Spheres*).

for an interesting worship visual, you could have several people placed on a stage or around a meeting room draw such circles on large boards or sheets of paper during a song.

To make a smaller, simpler version of the more complex experiment above, provide members of the group with small pieces of glass (e.g., a photo frame with the backing card removed and the glass glued to the frame) and permanent markers in a variety of colors. Let them scribble all over one side of the glass (which will have the same playful, out-of-control effect as the wax-melting) and practice their circles in a different color on the other side.

THE MEETING

1. How did you feel before drawing your first circle? How did you feel after?

2. Why do you think circles are a shape most people find pleasing?

3. Why do you think we like the idea of something being perfect?

4. If you did the more complex version, describe the way you felt while drawing and the way you felt while melting the wax. How much control did you have of the pen? the wax? How did you feel about things being less than perfect? At what other times have you had similar feelings? How are the two sides of the glass like two sides of life?

5. We long for perfection in the form of Heaven and the person of God. But how do we seek that perfection without becoming control freaks in our daily lives? What about being a perfectionist can cause us to miss out on God's perfection?

6. In what areas of life are you seeking a better situation, wishing for an ideal? How can this experiment help you be OK with your current situation or at least your lack of control over it?

7. How can you follow Solomon's advice to be happy, do good, find satisfaction, and let God be God?

eternity

TAKING IT TO THE STREET

Arthur Stace was known to many as "Mr. Eternity." After years of crime and alcoholism, his life was changed in 1930 when he heard a sermon about eternity and wanted to share it with his city. So, for years, he would rise early, take a box of chalk out to the streets of Sydney and simply write the word *eternity* on bus shelters, billboards, sidewalks. It's estimated that he wrote the word more than 500,000 times over the course of thirty-five years. While he tried to remain anonymous, he eventually became a legend in the city, to the point that for Sydney's New Year's Eve fireworks display of 2000, a huge "Eternity" lit up the famous Sydney Harbour Bridge (Australia's version of the Golden Gate), and this display was recreated later in the year for the opening of the Sydney Olympic Games. It could be said that he touched the city with eternity. While he didn't preach any sermon, he undoubtedly made millions think about the word *eternity* and what it held for them.

On a much simpler scale, you can touch your neighborhood with "eternity." Send a group out, armed with boxes of chalk for writing the word *eternity* on sidewalks, benches, even trash bins. (You may want to advise people to keep their writing on public spaces and on surfaces where the rain will easily wash the writing away.) If you do it very early in the morning and in enough places, it will begin to get people talking. If you want to be a little more poetic, try practicing your freehand circles all over the city too! When people see your marks in various places, they will be curious about what it means and who did it and how. Let there be some question about where it came from and how it's made. When word gets out that it was people from a church who were responsible, your community might see that Christians can be experimental and fun, that church is a place to explore ideas. For the individuals drawing the circles, the experience of drawing them in ordinary places might help them process what it means for them to be **OK with imperfection** while still looking to God's perfection in their daily lives.

Living the Double Life

"Even though I walk through the valley of the shadow of death,
I will fear no evil, for you are with me."

—PSALM 23:4

The Themes: perseverance, patience, encouragement, courage, faith, hope, life

The Reading: Psalm 23; Revelation 21:3, 4

THE THINKING

When was the last time you heard a sermon or read a devotional thought on Revelation? Preachers and writers avoid the book because it's like a bad dream—there's dragons and angels and blood. So we tell ourselves it's some kind of metaphor for the end of times and put it aside until then. But Revelation isn't so hard if we see the author, John, as both a doctor and an artist.

Let's start by examining the genre of the book: apocalyptic literature. Today *apocalyptic* has come to mean "catastrophic." But apocalyptic literature (the Greek word *apocalypsis* means simply "revelation," hence the name of the book) was a common genre, which people in the first century understood. "An apocalypse is defined as: 'a genre of revelatory literature with a narrative framework, in which a revelation is mediated by an otherworldly being to a human recipient, disclosing a transcendent reality which is both temporal, insofar as it envisages eschatological salvation, and spatial insofar as it involves another, supernatural world'" (John J. Collins, *The Apocalyptic Imagination*).

For us, the book of Revelation seems strange because it's the only book just like it that we know. (Although the Old Testament book of Daniel and parts of other books, such as Isaiah, Ezekiel, and 2 Thessalonians certainly have apocalyptic elements, but don't receive as much attention as Revelation.) But in fact, the full title of the book is "The Revelation of John" because there were "revelations" by others. All these writings take a similar form and were generally written to remind readers, often those undergoing tribulations, that there is a level of life beyond what they are currently experiencing, a place and time where they will be free, and at peace, with the aim that this will give them hope to persevere, that the peace might even begin now.

Imagine if you knew you had to undergo a medical procedure which involved five seconds of intense pain. Wouldn't the pain be easier to take if you were told ahead of time that it was only for five seconds? The pain is the same, either way, but if you know it has an end, it's endurable. In Revelation, John is our doctor, talking us through the pain, making it more sufferable by reminding us that it's finite. While that certainly has a future element—we're looking forward to the end of the pain—it is meant for the living, the suffering, the tormented, today. So if we set aside Revelation, we set aside all the encouragement it holds for us in the present.

Secondly, we need to be artists, not scientists, when we read Revelation. Too often readings of Revelation dissect each scene and assign each part a label. Instead, as you read it, allow John to paint an entire scene before you try to understand. If you've ever read a children's book with detailed illustrations, you'll know you can almost follow the story without reading the words. So think of Revelation as a picture book where the illustrations take shape in your head as you read. Ask someone else to read you a passage from Revelation (try 12:1-6) or use an audio version [see www.faithcomesbyhearing.com for a free audio Bible download] so that you can listen with your eyes closed. Allow a scene to build in your mind as you hear it described. Then "step back" to view it as a whole. Don't bother too much with the details or try to say "that character is Hitler" (or my neighbor), or "this is the millennial reign after the first rapture before the third tribulation." In each of the scenes, just ask questions like: Is there a good guy? Is there a bad guy? Does the good guy always seem to be winning? What happens to the good guy in the end? And what happens to the bad guy in the end?

Most of our favorite good guy/bad guy movies follow a similar formula: 1) Good Guy is strong; 2) Good Guy seems to be overthrown by Bad Guy; 3) Good Guy triumphs in the end. If the formula was 1) Good Guy is strong and 2) Good Guy triumphs in the end, it wouldn't be much of a story, would it? It wouldn't be believable to us because we live in a world of conflict. As much as we hate the trials of life, the stories of our lives are driven on by them. The best stories are not about the smooth sailing but the near misses. Life is full of paradoxes: on the one hand, we are happy, on the other hand, we have deep fears.

RECIPE FOR A MESS

On my way home from work each day, I drive up a steep hill. On one side of the road there's a view of the rundown part of town. On the other side, there's a small clearing in the woods. I've seen deer grazing there once or twice and it seemed so strange to see such natural beauty so close to the inner city. Now I make the choice every time I pass it to look for the deer. They're very rarely there, but the act of looking reminds me that it's good to choose to look for beauty, just like we choose to look for God in the ordinary. And on the rare occasions I do see the deer, it's a very special thing.

—A. L. S.

On the one hand, we are excited for the future, on the other hand, we know death is inevitable. Most good has some bad in it, and most bad has some good.

And John's life was no different. On the one hand, he was aware of God's provision, on the other hand, he was living in exile. On the one hand, he knew God's kingdom would be victorious, on the other hand, before his eyes God's kingdom was being torn apart by the Roman Empire (Revelation 1:9). To these people living in turmoil, or to us today, a pretty story would not ring true. So John uses paradoxes—situations where two opposites seem to coexist—to express the double-sided nature of the life of a Christian. It is a message which reminds us that, for God's people, all is not as it seems. We exist in a realm which hides the true nature of our existence: we seem to be losing, and yet we are winning; we seem to be overcome, and yet we are overcomers.

Let's look at a few examples: In Revelation 5:6-10 (*NASB*), we meet a Lamb, "standing, as if slain." Yet, is he weak and helpless? Then in Revelation 6:9-11 we're introduced to the martyrs under the altar. They're described as "slain because of the word of God" and they call for judgment of those who martyred them. Are they done for? (It's OK if you want to skip to the end— Revelation 20:4—to see how things work out for them.) Then John describes a strange scene where he is told to eat a scroll (10:9, 10). When he does, it is sweet as honey in his mouth and yet it makes his stomach bitter. Then a little later, in 12:1-6, we find a woman in labor and a huge, red dragon poised to devour her child, and we are sure the child is a goner. She and her child are extremely vulnerable and yet, to our amazement, at the last minute the child is caught up to God and the woman is whisked away to a place of safety in the wilderness.

These images catch our attention, cause us to ask questions: How can one being be both dead and alive? How can one thing be both sweet and bitter? How can one person be both incredibly vulnerable and yet safe? They're supposed to be confusing, because life is confusing. These images all remind us of the two sides of our experience: we also are dead yet living, crushed yet overcoming, vulnerable and yet saved. Our lives are also sweet yet bitter. These paradoxes show us that suffering in life does not mean God is not with us. Suffering is a normal part of the Christian's existence—indeed, of the human condition. Our hope is in freedom from this suffering and in the God who is waiting to welcome us into his arms.

Most of the paradoxes in Revelation are in the first twelve chapters. But as we continue to read Revelation, after the twelfth chapter the paradoxes become less and less frequent. God is overcoming the painful half of our experience. As we see in 21:3, 4, "He shall wipe away every tear from their eyes; and there shall no longer be any death; there shall no longer be any mourning, or crying or pain; the first things have passed away" (*NASB*). We will no longer be dead yet living, crushed yet overcoming, vulnerable yet saved. We will simply be living, overcoming, and saved. Amen! Come, Lord Jesus.

As I have come across signs of the paradoxes of life, I have collected these little pieces of evidence to encourage me in times when the dark side of the paradox is all I see. They serve as a reminder that I am not alone in my struggles—whoever wrote these lines was torn between loving and hating this world, like me. This is just a piece of my collection of prose, poetry, and hymn lyrics that reveal these paradoxes in life. The collection brings together writers from different times, places, and walks of life as a testimony to our shared experience of the double life.

On mourning yet singing

"My life flows on in endless song;
Above earth's lamentation
I hear the sweet though far off hymn
That hails a new creation:
Through all the tumult and the strife
I hear the music ringing;
It finds an echo in my soul—
How can I keep from singing?
What though my joys and comforts die?
The Lord my Savior liveth;
What though the darkness gather round!
Songs in the night He giveth:
No storm can shake my inmost calm
While to that refuge clinging;
Since Christ is Lord of Heav'n and earth,
How can I keep from singing?
I lift mine eyes; the cloud grows thin;
I see the blue above it;
And day by day this pathway smoothes
Since first I learned to love it:
The peace of Christ makes fresh my heart,
A fountain ever springing:
All things are mine since I am His—
How can I keep from singing?"

—Robert Lowry, "How Can I Keep from Singing?"

On being tormented yet peaceful

"When peace, like a river, attendeth my way,
When sorrows like sea billows roll;
Whatever my lot,
Thou hast taught me to say,
It is well, it is well with my soul.
. . .
Though Satan should buffet, tho' trials should come,
Let this blest assurance control,
That Christ has regarded my helpless estate,
And hath shed His own blood for my soul."
—Horatio G. Spafford, "It Is Well With My Soul"

On laughing yet crying

"To be both ironic and Christian is to know, with a knowing deeper than doctrine, the simple, unnerving truth that the visage of faith is not the happy face but the masks of comedy and tragedy, alternating, unpredictably, between laughter and tears, sometimes crying and laughing at the same time, or even, on occasion, crying because it's so funny and laughing because it hurts so much."
—Patrick Henry, *The Ironic Christian's Companion: Finding the Marks of God's Grace in the World*

On feeling forsaken yet obeying

"Do not be deceived, Wormwood. Our cause is never more in danger than when a human, no longer desiring,

but still intending, to do our Enemy's will, looks round upon a universe from which every trace of Him seems to have vanished, and asks why he has been forsaken, and still obeys."
—The demon, Screwtape, in a letter to his nephew, Wormwood, a novice demon, from C. S. Lewis, *The Screwtape Letters*

On grieving yet dancing
"There is a time for everything, and a season for every activity under heaven . . . a time to weep and a time to laugh, a time to mourn and a time to dance."
—Ecclesiastes 3:1, 4

On being oppressed yet persevering

THE MAKING

Experiment 6a

Keep your own scrapbook or journal as a collection of **evidence** of the double-sided life. Record any time you hear or see signs that we're all in this strange existence together—whether it's a quote from a movie, a line from a song, a photo, or a clipping from the newspaper. The collection, over time, will remind you that you are not alone, that others are writing, singing, talking about this strange life, and the act of collecting will keep your eyes open to those **reminders**.

Experiment 6b

To get started, read passages from Revelation 5:6-10; 6:9-11; 10:9, 10; 12:1-6 and take note of the parts of each scene which **represent** good and bad things. John is an artist, painting scenes, and he uses juxtaposition to allow the two sides of life to stand in contrast. Artists use **juxtaposition** to allow two or more objects to comment on each other, just as a shirt emblazoned with the words "Perfect Princess" will highlight any time the wearer behaves in a way which is imperfect or unfitting for a princess. Just as a homeless man who sits on the steps of an expensive boutique highlights its opulence by his very (grimy) presence.

Now reflect on **what represents hope**, blessing, safety, and peace in your life. Find some evidence of this, whether a memento from vacation or something made by your grandchild. On the other hand, what represents suffering, trials, hopelessness? Find an item which represents the challenges and hardships, perhaps a death certificate or gift from an estranged friend. These items may mean nothing to anyone else. They may be significant only because of what they represent to you. Arrange the two items, side by side, and photograph them, juxtaposing **evidence** of blessings with **evidence** of challenges. Choose your favorite photos, print them and frame them, or add them to a scrapbook (see above).

MAKING IT WORK FOR SMALL GROUPS OR CORPORATE WORSHIP SETTINGS

Since individual journals or scrapbooks may take some time, after doing the study of Revelation, ask each person to bring with them next time one piece of evidence of the double-sided nature of life. Allow time during your next meeting for the group to share their stories or clippings, or make a group scrapbook.

THE MEETING

1. What are the biggest challenges you face in life?

2. Even if you've never been persecuted for your faith, all trials can challenge our faith in God. How have the trials in your life challenged your faith?

3. Did this experiment change your approach to your challenges? If so, how? How has it allowed you to be more aware of the fact that challenges and trials will pass, and that good will live on eternally?

4. How do you feel about your connections to others, knowing that this double-sided life is a life we all share? How can this awareness help you to connect to strangers or people with whom you may have broken relationships?

5. How can this experiment help you to feel more gratitude in your life?

TAKING IT TO THE STREET

Ask group members to bring cameras or provide disposable cameras and take the group out for an impromptu walk. Ask them to find signs of beauty coexisting with brokenness or order coexisting with chaos—a smiling child with a broken arm or a flower growing through a crack in the concrete—and photograph them. Exhibit your findings at a group art show.

Note: This Experiment was adapted from my essay, "Living the Double Life: Revealing Revelation's Paradoxes" in Christ's Victorious Church: Essays on Biblical Ecclesiology and Eschatology in Honor of Tom Friskney, *Jon A. Weatherly, ed., Wipf and Stock Publishers, 2001.*

"Christians should be those least threatened of all by new artistic ideas, by experimentation, by taking risks, by looking at and enjoying what the other side has to say. If indeed our feet are solidly rooted on truth itself, we are those who can look the world in the eye with confidence, pleasure, fulfilment."

—Franky Schaeffer, *Addicted to Mediocrity: 20th Century Christians and the Arts*

Experiment 6 65

BLURRING THE SECULAR/SACRED DIVIDE

*"So whether you eat or drink or whatever you do,
do it all for the glory of God."*

—1 Corinthians 10:31

Once I owned a piece of exercise equipment, and it was the first time I'd ever owned, or even ever heard of, a fitness gadget whose name included the word *lounge*. The "As-Seen-on-TV Ab Lounge" looks like the bones of a recliner whose bolts are all loose so that sitting in it requires the use of "core muscles." This Ab Lounge will add to my collection of furniture that acts like exercise equipment, that acts like furniture (which already includes a rather wobbly office chair in the form of a huge rubber exercise ball). So now I ask myself, am I working out while watching TV or watching TV while working out? I like the idea that these pieces of furniture-slash-workout-equipment blur that line between exertion and relaxation. And one day, as I was trying out my new gadget, hovering in that nowhere land between the two extremes, I had a revelation.

At a local bookstore we see the Inspirational sign, dividing books into secular and sacred, and it's easy to retain that distinction in our lives. But was it God or some marketing guru who came up with the secular/sacred divide? We put ministry, Bible study, VeggieTales, and worship songs into the "spiritual" basket and everything else into the "secular" basket. That means that the spiritual basket holds just a few things and everything else belongs to the world. We've painted ourselves into a tiny corner and made ourselves afraid of whatever lies beyond it.

But so-called secular things can be meaningful to Christians because they may evoke beauty and so lead us to the creator of beauty. They may help us understand the circumstances of others; they may give us hope. There are some things created by the world which glorify the ugliness and emptiness, but there are others which would agree with us that the world cannot fill all our longings. I must admit that I've had more spiritual moments reading Umberto Ecco and Chaim Potok than Frank Peretti. Secular movies have revealed great truth to me, in spite of, or even because of, their more gritty scenes. And I certainly find more transcendent moments in the music of Nikolai Rimsky-Korsakov than in anything recorded by Amy Grant. Should I feel guilty that Matisse and the ocean stir more awe in me than Thomas Kinkade does? Because many of these works in which I find inspiration wouldn't be caught dead in the Inspirational department.

I get the feeling that Paul knew about the essence of this issue. He knew the intention of the heart was what decides the secular or sacred status of the things we consume. He takes care in his first letter to the Corinthians to talk about the

RECIPE FOR A MESS

In our city there's an old market which has been there since around the time of the Civil War. I find that shopping there is an entirely different experience from visiting the chain-store supermarkets. This market draws people from all over the city (and the world) and sells handmade crafts and homegrown fruits and flowers, so I am able to see the color and diversity of God's creation. Usually there are musicians performing, sometimes jazz saxophone, sometimes African drums, so there's a rhythm and noise to the place. And the people who run the stalls have often grown or made the products, and this gives me a greater connection to God's earth. When I take home the food I buy there and prepare it for my family, I feel that my family becomes a part of that bigger vision of our colorful world.

—M. L. P.

> *"I make myself a slave to everyone, to win as many as possible. To the Jews I became like a Jew, to win the Jews. To those under the law I became like one under the law (though I myself am not under the law), so as to win those under the law. To those not having the law I became like one not having the law (though I am not free from God's law but am under Christ's law), so as to win those not having the law. To the weak I became weak, to win the weak. I have become all things to all men so that by all possible means I might save some. I do all this for the sake of the gospel, that I may share in its blessings."*
> —1 Corinthians 9:19-23

issue in detail—though he discusses meat instead of movies. The question had arisen in Corinth about whether Christians could eat meat that had been sacrificed to idols. One might expect Paul to say "Absolutely not! Have nothing to do with these pagan practices!" But instead he explains how, based on the believer's previous experiences, one piece of meat could be at the same time the embodiment of evil to one believer and to another, a wholesome provision from God. I imagine that first-century butcher shops didn't have secular and sacred meat sections, so Paul allowed Christians to decide for themselves, based on whether the consumption of that meat reminded them of all things unnatural and evil, or all things godly and good.

I've not heard many heated small group discussions lately on the ethics of idol meat, but issues like how a Christian chooses movies, books, music, even friends and employment does find its way into such discussions on a regular basis, because we are sometimes able to find hints of truth and light, even in spite of the author's intention, in the most unexpected places. If there was some way you were led to God while reading the latest bestseller or listening to the radio, for you that book and that music have become spiritual. And it doesn't stop with our selections from the bookstore, but filters into every area of our lives. When we do our work with service in mind, our work has become as spiritual as any work done by Mother Teresa, even if it's just flipping burgers. And when we carry on conversations with our calling in mind, our words carry as much weight as any uttered by Billy Graham. Even by asking ourselves "How can my haircut communicate the right message about Christ?" and "How can I choose a car which glorifies God?" we can make seemingly mundane, secular choices deeply spiritual—just as thinking hateful thoughts about the woman two pews away while singing "I Love You, Lord" suddenly makes that worship moment intensely *un*spiritual.

As usual, Paul has the perfect summary for such a complex topic. He finishes his discussion to the Corinthians with "Whatever you eat or drink or whatever you do, you must do all for the glory of God." He saw that, for different people from different backgrounds, giving glory to God takes different forms. He knew that, to find God in the ordinary, we may have to stretch the boundaries of where we expect to find him. And this message is as timely today as when Paul first penned it. But maybe for our purposes, we could say: "Whatever you do, whether you tattoo your body for the sake of being relevant to alternative nonbelievers or wear a suit for the sake of being approachable to your conservative workmates, do all for the glory of God. Whether you listen to Third Day, Third Eye Blind, or Rachmaninoff's Third Piano Concerto, do all for the glory of God. Whether you read J. K. Rowling, J. I. Packer, or P. J. O'Rourke, do all for the glory of God."

TAKE A MOMENT

1. How much do you chop the world and your life into spiritual and secular? Try to be conscious of this as you go through a week. Why do you think you categorize things the way that you do?

2. As an exercise, find opportunities to make watching the news, buying groceries, or getting a haircut a spiritual thing. What parts of your experiences lend themselves to being spiritual more than others?

3. On the flipside of that, make a list of things we label as unquestionably (usually) spiritual. Going to church? Singing worship songs? In what ways do you feel these things can become secular? How can that affect your own faith or that of others?

If Only

"As you do not know the path of the wind, or how the body is formed in a mother's womb,
so you cannot understand the work of God, the Maker of all things."
—ECCLESIASTES 11:5

The Themes: wishing, dissatisfaction, hope, resignation, happiness, control, contentment, peace
The Reading: Ecclesiastes 9:7-10; 11:5

THE THINKING

As children we see through untainted eyes, imagining the world can fulfill all our hopes and longings. We spend the first twenty or thirty years of our lives attaining all our childhood dreams—the degree, the relationships, the career, the house, the kids, the dog. But beyond them we find still more dreams left to fill. As we mature, and find our longings still unsatisfied, we gradually begin to wonder if this world can ever be enough. No matter how much money, love, happiness, success, health, good luck, and beauty you might manage to amass, it will eventually let you down, one way or another. Money is spent, lost, or, even if it's invested wisely, passes on to someone else when we die. All our earthly relationships are with fallible humans who will eventually leave, whether by choice or simple mortality. And we all know the fickleness of things such as success, health, and good luck. Our happiness hangs on very tenuous threads. But all this is old news. Thousands of years ago King Solomon wrote Ecclesiastes to express how, in spite of all his wealth and influence, he felt totally powerless. And, like Solomon, on a daily basis, whether we're trying to stop the cat from clawing the couch or waiting to be cured from cancer, we feel powerless over our situations in life.

Whether we express our longings with words or simply through our choices, we all long for something. Something more or something else, something we cannot have. Just as the most perfect piece of pie is spoiled by a visit from one, tiny fly, even in a full and happy life, we are distracted by the one thing that is not right. We look in the mirror and think "if only." We trudge to the office and murmur "if only." We visit a dying friend and say "if only." How does your heart say "if only"? What lack do you feel that mars the peace and perfection? (Stop here and do Part 1 of The Making, below.)

Remember a time when you did get the thing you were wishing for. Was it all you hoped for? Even if it lived up to all your expectations, did it keep you from having other "if only" wishes? As soon as you got the house you wished for, you longed for a different car. As soon as you found the spouse you wanted, you wished they would understand you better.

Solomon realizes that the answer isn't found in having all you want but in accepting two simple but life-changing truths: "I'm not in control" and "It's never enough." Solomon describes the effort to control the world as a chasing after the wind. He paints the image of a desperate man, exerting all his efforts to catch the moving air around him. But if you know anything about wind, you know it will not be tamed. The thought of expending energy on trying to catch it is ridiculous.

We can choose to spend our lives in a comic effort to fill our pockets with handfuls of wind. Or we can choose to befriend the wind and learn its changing ways.

WE CAN LEARN TO FLY A KITE. WE CAN LEARN TO SAY:

"GOD IS IN CONTROL"
AND
"GOD IS ENOUGH."

There are two levels of life—the one we can't control and the one we can. Oddly enough, we can only exercise control by choosing to be OK with the fact that we have no control. We can brace ourselves and wince all the way through the roller coaster ride. Or we can loosen up and enjoy it. (Now do Part 2 of The Making.)

THE MAKING

Gather these materials:

- 🔘 a canvas board or piece of poster board, approximately 12 by 18 inches (Or look in a salvage yard or junk shop for an old door or panel—anything flat, clean, and able to take acrylic paint.)
- 🔘 fine- or medium-point permanent markers
- 🔘 acrylic paints, in a variety of colors
- 🔘 paper towels and water for washing hands
- 🔘 painting utensils such as brushes, straws, or sponges
- 🔘 newspaper or drop cloth to protect the workspace

Part 1

Take some time to reflect on the area of your life in which you feel the most "if only" thoughts. Do you long for something else in your relationships? in your work? in your living situation? in your financial, physical, spiritual, or emotional life?

For an interesting twist, instead of using a flat piece of board or panel, find a wooden or cardboard box with a lid. Make sure it's large enough to write inside (around the size of a small shoe box would be ideal). Do Part 1 of the experiment on the inside of the box and Part 2 on the outside of the box. This will help express the two levels of life in a different way.

Fill the board or sheet of paper with thoughts and feelings related to "if only" thinking. If you have issues with your body, write or draw the changes you'd make if you could or the attributes you don't like about yourself, or draw your ideal self. If you long for an end to your work, write your daily "to do" list. If you'd like a better job, write a job description for your perfect job. If you'd like a different family situation, write a letter you'd like to receive from the person you'd like to add to your family (or a letter of reconciliation you'd like to receive from the one who is estranged from you). If you'd like a better house, draw or describe it. Or just complete the sentence "If only . . ." and write out your thoughts till the words fill the page.

It's OK to be honest here. This isn't about writing the thoughts you probably *should* have, but how you actually feel. But don't worry; this phase is only the beginning.

Take a minute to pray—admit those feelings and longings to God.

Part 2

Squirt the paints onto the page or board on which you were writing in Part 1, roll up your sleeves, and do some finger-painting. Resist the urge to make a particular shape, just play. Experiment with other methods. For example, water down the paint a little and hold the paper up to let it drip down the page. Or, using the watered-down paint again, blow it with a straw and see where it goes. Or, if you're feeling energetic, soak a sponge in paint and throw it at the paper. Just mess around with different ways to play and give up control of the paint. Now look at the interesting patterns your paint has made. If you like, when it's dry, cut or fold it into a kite shape. Or if you cannot fold or cut the material, you could outline a kite shape.

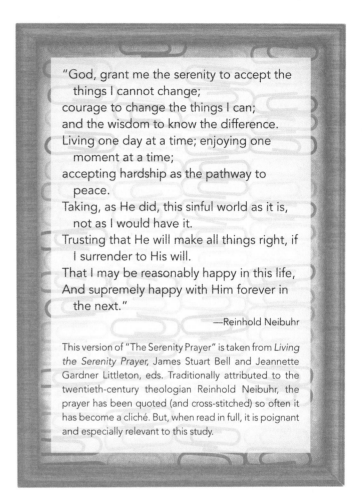

"God, grant me the serenity to accept the things I cannot change;
courage to change the things I can;
and the wisdom to know the difference.
Living one day at a time; enjoying one moment at a time;
accepting hardship as the pathway to peace.
Taking, as He did, this sinful world as it is, not as I would have it.
Trusting that He will make all things right, if I surrender to His will.
That I may be reasonably happy in this life, And supremely happy with Him forever in the next."

—Reinhold Neibuhr

This version of "The Serenity Prayer" is taken from *Living the Serenity Prayer*, James Stuart Bell and Jeannette Gardner Littleton, eds. Traditionally attributed to the twentieth-century theologian Reinhold Neibuhr, the prayer has been quoted (and cross-stitched) so often it has become a cliché. But, when read in full, it is poignant and especially relevant to this study.

MAKING IT WORK FOR SMALL GROUPS OR CORPORATE WORSHIP SETTINGS

In a group setting, be sure to provide plenty of time and space for individuals to explore their "if only" thoughts. Perhaps give them a few minutes of small group discussion time to help them develop their ideas before beginning the experiment. Make sure to warn people beforehand about getting paint on their clothes and do the exercise outside or protect the workspace. Either plan the activity near a sink where people can easily wash their hands or provide buckets of water and towels.

If this group is going through a time of change and needs to deal with it as a community, allow them to do a group experiment, writing all their thoughts and painting together on one large piece.

" Life is too important to be taken seriously."

—adapted from a line written by Oscar Wilde for two of his plays, *Vera* and *Lady Windemere's Fan*, from *Complete Works of Oscar Wilde*

RECIPE FOR A MESS

I feel God in the unexpected. There are so many times I feel as though I'm praying for the impossible . . . and then the impossible happens!

—N. B.

If the group is very large, such as in a church service, you could have everyone write down their "if only" thoughts on scraps of paper and then collect those. Have one person (either an artistic person or not) write these statements on a large board in front of the group as the service is going on. He or she can then paint over the surface and leave the display (whether kite-shaped or not) up for everyone to see. This could be a great visual for a talk on contentment or control.

THE MEETING

1. Did it feel good to name the "if only" thoughts you have? Was it difficult?

2. After taking the time to play, do you feel any different about your desire to control the aspect of your life that you wrote about? What did the painting experiment physically do to the thoughts you first wrote down? What did the painting experiment mentally do to the thoughts you first wrote down?

3. How can you enjoy a life which will never be free from "if onlys"? What steps can you take to feel closer to being OK with the statements "God is enough" or "God is in control"?

4. In the particular situation you wrote about or are thinking of, how can God be enough? How is God in control? How could playfulness and resignation help you let go of that situation a little?

Note: This experiment is based on my book Life Is Too Important to Be Taken Seriously: Kite-Flying Lessons from Ecclesiastes, *published by College Press.*

TAKING IT TO THE STREET

Go kite-flying.

EXPERIMENT 8

Self-Portrait

"I praise you because I am fearfully and wonderfully made;
your works are wonderful, I know that full well."

—Psalm 139:14

The Themes: creation, beauty, uniqueness, signs of God
The Reading: Psalm 8; 139:13-16

THE THINKING

I was thirty-four before I discovered my best feature. My daughter and I were reading a book about the human body, and when we got to the page describing the different patterns of fingerprints, of course we had to study our own. And we discovered that hidden in my left index fingerprint was a perfect spiral.

After overcoming my disappointment that I live in a culture where fingerprint perfection is underappreciated, I decided to share my discovery with the world in a painting entitled *Self-Portrait*. As I carefully reproduced the swirls and traces of my own fingerprint, I couldn't help but reflect on the personal touches our creator had added to each one of us. Why did he see fit to give us each unique prints? I'm sure he had more in mind than the identification of criminals. Perhaps he liked the thought that we would leave our own special mark on everything and everyone we touched. Literally.

THE MAKING

Gather these materials:

- small canvas or board (An oval or rectangle probably lends itself best to the proportions of a fingerprint. Any size will work, however, the larger the canvas is, the more difficult it will be to copy a tiny fingerprint.)
- pencil
- acrylic paints
- thin paintbrushes (approximately ¼ inch thick or smaller)
- magnifying glass (optional)
- ink pad and paper (optional)

I left the canvas white and painted my print in a thick, black line, however, you can experiment with different colors for both the background and the fingerprint. If you paint the background, be sure it is dry before working on the fingerprint. Be sure to have good light and start in the center (of both your finger and the canvas) and work out, a section at a time, until you fill the entire canvas. It may be easier to see if you use a magnifying glass or if you make an ink fingerprint to copy from. You can start with a pencil and paint over it later. It doesn't matter if the lines don't exactly match your print. It's an interesting exercise to realize how complicated one tiny fingertip is and to consider how much more complex a digestive system or spinal cord might be. To keep the experiment

One practice I've begun in the past few years in order to counter my negative, critical, initial reactions to wrongdoing, foolishness, thoughtlessness, or just plain sin, is to pray for that person or situation. It comes from Paul's command to not worry about anything but pray for everything with thanksgiving (Philippians 4:6). When I pick up litter, instead of being angry with the selfish person who threw out that bottle, I can pray for the litterer, since God knows who that person is! The item has fingerprints that God recognizes.

—A. E.

RECIPE FOR A MESS

Check out the (only slightly cheesy) mini-documentary called "The Fingerprints of God" on the YouTube site (http://www.youtube.com/watch?v=-lbc8sD5sgw&feature=related).

Perform a Google search on the name "Chuck Close" to see work by this American artist who uses fingerprints to paint huge faces (especially one of an older lady called Fanny).

When you first look at a Chuck Close fingerprint painting it looks slightly pixelated, which, in our digital world, seems like something impersonal, the product of a machine. And yet, on closer examination, you see that each tiny dot is a human fingerprint.

from becoming an exercise in navel (or finger) gazing alone, reflect on the **INTRICACIES** in God's creation—how **IMMENSE YET DETAILED** it is, what one fingerprint reveals about him.

Another option—rather than doing just one large canvas, try painting five small canvases, one for each fingerprint on **ONE HAND**. And instead of signing your name in the lower corner of the painting or paintings, sign it with an imprint of the original fingerprint, in a different color (although it will be the mirror image of what you have painted).

If you're up for more of a challenge, try copying the details of the iris (the colored part) of an **EYE**—yours or someone else's—on a large scale. Iris scanners are used as a form of identification, because, like fingerprints, each person's iris is **UNIQUE**.

MAKING IT WORK FOR SMALL GROUPS OR CORPORATE WORSHIP SETTINGS

Invite individuals to paint "portraits" of others' fingerprints. Or, after having each person do five small images of all the prints on their own hand, invite the group to swap so that at the end each person has a "hand" (a collection of five prints) made up of different people's prints.

For a large group exercise, you could set up a counter or table with several inkpads and sheets of paper near the entryway of your setting. Also be sure to provide hand wipes so people can clean off the ink. Invite people to make fingerprints of just one of their fingers and have them write their names beside their prints. All of these images could then be scanned or photographed and compiled in a digital slideshow presentation which could be shown during a worship service that is themed around God's creation.

Fingerprint Trivia

Scientists are not sure exactly why we have fingerprints. Recent studies have found that, contrary to popular opinion, they don't help with grip. Rather, they seem to make our fingertips more flexible and sensitive. (see http://bodyodd.msnbc.msn.com/archive/2009/06/23/1975088.aspx)

Some animals have fingerprints—mostly tree-climbing animals. And there's a monkey in South America which has similar prints on its tail! (see http://bodyodd.msnbc.msn.com/archive/2009/06/23/1975088.aspx)

Did you know that koalas have individual fingerprints like humans? (see https://www.savethekoala.com/koalasphysic.html)

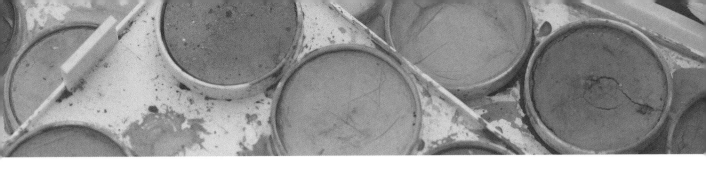

THE MEETING

1. Have you ever looked closely at your own fingerprints before? Are your fingerprints the same on both hands? What do you notice about them?

2. What did you learn from doing this exercise? Were you surprised by anything?

3. As you painted, did you reflect on God's creation? What did you discover? Why do you think we have fingerprints? What do you find interesting about God's attention to details?

TAKING IT TO THE STREET

Ask a local café or coffee shop if they would allow you to have a group display of the fingerprints. If possible, provide a small sign describing the project. Include comments from the artists if you like.

Go for a walk and examine the intricacies of other parts of nature—the tiny patterns on a leaf or in tree bark.

Elements of Making and Meeting

THE MEANING OF ART AND METAPHOR

"This is what God the LORD says—he who created the heavens and stretched them out, who spread out the earth and all that comes out of it, who gives breath to its people, and life to those who walk on it."
—ISAIAH 42:5

Minute-by-minute, minutiae-by-minutiae. The prevalence of texting, Twittering, and Facebooking has shown us how much we yearn to share our ideas, feelings, and beliefs with one another. And not only do we want to tell about ourselves, we want to share our favorite photos, music, movies, and books with each other. Because the dry list of facts is not enough. Performance artist, Philippe Petit, put it simply: "Truth deserves more than being factually recorded" (as quoted by Steven Garrett, "Warner Herzog Walks the Rope," *Esquire Magazine*). This is why we need the arts.

I've never met the painter Gustav Klimt, but I feel I know something about him because his paintings express a complex, romantic character. I've never met the musician Sting, but I feel I know him a little because his songs express emotional sensitivity, and maybe a little cynicism. Although we may not know lifeless data like their

"The artistic impulse is universal. . . . Painting something that comes from within fulfills a genuine need."
—Susan Striker, *The Anti-Coloring Book*

dates of birth or addresses, we all feel a connection to actors and musicians, artists and writers because we've seen their art, experienced their metaphors. Isn't this something like the kind of connection we'd like to have with God? Wouldn't we like our relationship to be based on more than knowing his vital statistics?

We all are moved by metaphors, even when we're unaware of it, even in the middle of ordinary days. A few years ago on a road trip, we got stuck in a traffic jam that stretched as far as the eye could see in both directions. Not only did we have the usual frustration of gridlock, we had the additional aggravation of having to inch along right beside a perfectly clear, perfectly usable strip of road. The construction company had set up miles of barrels to keep the traffic in one lane but nothing was happening in the closed lane. The first fifteen minutes of sitting produced the usual expressions of annoyance and anxiety. However, as time wore on and we knew we weren't getting anywhere anytime soon, resignation settled in. So each time the car ahead edged forward, instead of zooming to keep up, my husband began to slowly weave the car across the two lanes, in and out through the barrels—a simple statement of the ridiculousness of our situation and of our resignation to it. Of course, this was fun for the occupants of our car but the best part came when we looked behind us to see twenty or thirty cars behind us joining in, like a great long line of elephants. We never saw the faces of those in the cars behind us, and never will, but we all had a moment of making fun out of frustration, of enjoying our common humanness.

Metaphors transport rather than tell. If the other drivers had all popped their heads out and hollered "We're all in this

together" or "Let's make the most of this situation," we wouldn't have felt it half as strongly as we did while moseying together along that highway. Of course, God knows the power of metaphor. He could write "I'm with you" in black letters across a plain white sky every morning, but he chose the better way: to set a sphere of warmth and light in motion to begin each day. He could have organized for babies to appear on demand, but instead he made it so that two people would become one in order to create a new being which had characteristics of both of them, as a physical representation of their oneness. In fact, since we are "like or as" him, perhaps it could be said that we, ourselves, are similes. It would seem that for an unseen, otherworldly God to connect with beings in our realm, he needs to be fluent in metaphor. And he is.

"I am your shield, your very great reward" (Genesis 15:1).

"I am . . . the bright Morning Star" (Revelation 22:16).

"How often I have longed to gather your children together, as a hen gathers her chicks under her wings" (Matthew 23:37).

TAKE A M⊙MENT

1. Recall a time when a metaphor moved you. Was it in a story or movie? A wedding ceremony or funeral? Was it something you watched or something you were a part of? What made it meaningful? What did it represent in your life? How did you respond to it?

2. Consider normal parts of your life which may be metaphors you've never recognized. Is there a metaphor hidden in your sleeping, washing, working, cooking, traveling, eating? Does seeing these as metaphors make them more meaningful?

3. Is there a feeling or belief you would like to express to God, yourself, or a loved one? What metaphor could you use to express it?

4. If the idea of creating metaphors bamboozles you, consider your most vivid dreams. Your subconscious is an art director, creating big-budget movies every night. Without even thinking about it, you nightly cast nakedness for vulnerability, flying for freedom, fleeing for fear. Take a moment to make notes of the most poignant metaphors your dreams have created. If you can do it in your sleep, imagine what you can do when you try! Scripture is also an excellent source for metaphors: baptism for a change of heart, Communion for community, light for truth. Consider the many metaphors in Scripture and find one you could play out in your life to communicate to God.

So if God gets metaphor and humans can get metaphor, how can we use this language to communicate with him and with each other? We have so many ideas and beliefs we long to express, but we are limited and afraid. This year I saw this in a new way at a retreat. I had been invited to lead the weekend, and my sister and her son came along. On the Saturday afternoon, I took him to the retreat's art center. A large canvas and paints were spread out in the cool of a shade tree, and it seemed like the perfect place to while away an hour, having messy fun with a two-year-old. But the art center wasn't fun for everyone. During that hour, five or six other adults visited and every single one of them began with something like "I'm not very artistic," and then proceeded to force out what they hoped looked like something and left, feeling less for it.

That night as I prepared for the next day's final session, I knew I had to radically change my plans—I had an art activity planned for this group of people who seemed afraid of the very idea of art! So my final session began with a firm reminder: Forget about how it looks! Think about what it represents to you.

To my amazement, this same group, who had faced the art center with grimaces, dove into this art activity with joy. We reflected back on the lessons of the weekend and created metaphors for the changes we would make in our lives. Our minds had learned during sessions of listening and talking, and now our hands and hearts had their turn. We

RECIPE FOR A MESS

God has many languages. Some people speak to God through prayer, or music, or knowledge. The language of God that I speak most fluently is that of nature. When God created the place in which he desired to have a relationship with humanity, it was not a temple, but a garden. . . .

—R. S.

set our paintings outside to dry and went out later to find that the wind had blown some away. But, rather than a bother, this was an opportunity to see how effective the exercise had been in transporting souls through metaphor. As one woman went searching for her art project, I overheard her say, "It doesn't really matter to me if I find the hard copy, because now the art is in me."

So, what's the secret to the power and meaning of the arts? Why was that art project able to communicate something that the teaching and small group sessions hadn't? It's no small task to ask, or to answer: What is art? Is it beauty? If so, then why don't we put Sophia Loren and autumn leaves in art galleries? For me, and for many, art is more than beauty. It's a form of communication, as sculptor Anne Truitt recognizes when she describes her motivation to make art as a "passion for learning how to make true for others what I felt to be true for myself" (*Daybook: The Journal of an Artist*).

Good art is not necessarily beautiful. Good art is art that naturally communicates its message, moving the viewer without effort or explanation, whether it be a statement about politics or nature, and whether it be expressed with vibrant red oils or the right placement of a piece of clay. But where does that leave us—ordinary people who have a desire to make something and say something, people who haven't had the artistic advantage of hippie parents or years of art school? Are we able to make "good" art, art that gets across a message?

In recent years, art has become a popular form of expressing worship. And why not? As we've seen, God gets symbols. From circumcision to dragons, Scripture seems to reveal his penchant for metaphor. And, of course, he gets design. One look at a shell or a human hand, and we see the touch of a master designer. So it seems only right that we want to make beautiful and symbolic creations for our creator.

"The light shines in the darkness, but the darkness has not understood it." Jn 1.5

But what if we're just not very good at making things? Does being less creative make us less like the creator? Sadly, we live in a world which says "What is it?" to children instead of "Oh! I love the way that blue blob melts into the red squiggles!" And so after many years of having to explain what it is, we give up. We're all artists when we're five, but by the time we reach ten, we believe only the chosen few are good at art. We put aside an entire chunk of our vocabulary for talking to God—and become oblivious to an entire vocabulary he uses to talk to us.

But the lovely loophole in making art for God is that, if good art is art that communicates, when your audience can read your mind and knows your heart, all art is good. All art is meaningful when God is the art critic. As artist Mark Rothko passionately believed, the work of art depends for its very life on the attitude of the one who owns it. "In the hands of someone who did not respond to it, or who treated it simply as a financial investment, a picture would actually, he felt, be diminished, its very life drained out of it; whereas in the home of an appreciative owner it would continue to grow, infused with new life and vitality" (Edward Robinson, *The Language of Mystery*). We can be assured that the One who "owns" our art will certainly be an appreciative owner, in both the sense of understanding and valuing our gift.

In other words, we are freed to create. Whether or not it could hang in the Louvre is irrelevant. A child, when painting a messy masterpiece for her mother, doesn't ask if it's good enough. She thinks of her mom and wants to make her something and so she does. And her mom loves it. And her mom "gets" it. So think of something you want to say to your God. And say it to him. Don't focus on how good it is. And don't focus on the end product—the process is just as important. This isn't to say that the process of making art will always be moving and meaningful. Sometimes it's just plain messy and monotonous. But it is, nonetheless, a gift to God. Not only does he get symbols and colors and design, he also gets failure.

"Every child is an artist. The problem is how to remain an artist after he grows up."

—Roger von Oech, *A Kick in the Seat of the Pants*

TAKE A MOMENT

PLAYFULNESS helps us lose the fear that our work might not be good enough. Here are a few exercises to help rediscover playfulness. (If you have any children on hand, get them involved—they're experts at being creative and having fun.)

1. While few adults draw or paint regularly, we all write, and so this might be a good way to reintroduce ourselves to artistic expression. Try writing the following words in styles and colors which seem fitting to the word:

   GLASS. POINT. FEAR. LOUD. SIGH. GLANCE. BUMP. BOX. SHORE. BROWN. COMPUTER.

2. Take out a blank sheet of paper or a lump of clay (play clay or dough will do). Observe its blankness for a minute and visualize something very simple you'd like to do with it—like scrunch it into a ball, make a big X on it, or flatten it into a pancake. Consider that that image in your mind is about to make its debut in the real world. Your idea is about to be transformed into something concrete. Now do it. Imagine something new you can do. Do it again.

3. Open a junk drawer or cupboard of sundry things or flip to a random page of a magazine—anywhere that promises to offer a smorgasbord of shapes and colors. What stands out to you? If you had to choose one thing, what would you choose? Why? Did you like the way it looks or did you want to see how it would feel? Maybe you were just annoyed because it wasn't straight or was in the wrong place? Becoming sensitive to our senses is a big part of awakening our creative side.

4. As a child, growing up in Australia, one of my favorite TV shows was Mr. Squiggle, a marionette with a large pencil for a nose. Each week, children sent in "squiggles"—random arrangements of shapes and doodles on a sheet of paper—and with his large, pencil nose he would miraculously turn three circles and a square into a seal juggling ice cream cones. Have a friend draw random shapes/lines for you and see what you can make with them. (You can hold the pencil in your hand, though.)

5. Tear or cut colored paper into random shapes. Arrange the shapes into designs/images. Don't start with a finished image in mind—just start playing with the pieces and see what happens. If something doesn't look right, rearrange it. If it does look right, what about it seems right to you and why? Is it right because it's tidy and symmetrical or because it has interesting color and line combinations?

6. Take a sharp, lead pencil and piece of thin paper (printer paper should work) and find textures around you. Leaves, wall textures, the soles of your shoes, a corduroy jacket, and coins all provide interesting textures. Lay the piece of paper on the textured item and rub over it with your pencil (lay the pencil on its side and use the broad edge of the lead). The textures may show up differently on paper than you had expected. Spend some time collecting texture rubbings, and as you do, you may find that you look at ordinary things in a new way. Instead of seeing their colors or thinking of their uses, you may start to notice textures and shapes all around you.

For more ideas and creativity exercises, check out the following books:

○ *The Book of Think*: *Or How to Solve a Problem Twice Your Size*, by Marilyn Burns

○ *A Kick in the Seat of the Pants*, by Roger von Oech

○ *The New Drawing on the Right Side of the Brain,* by Betty Edwards

"The mechanism by which spirituality becomes passionate is metaphor. An ineffable God requires metaphor not only to be imagined but to be approached, exhorted, evaded, confronted, struggled with, and loved."

—George Lakoff and Mark Johnson, *Philosophy in the Flesh*

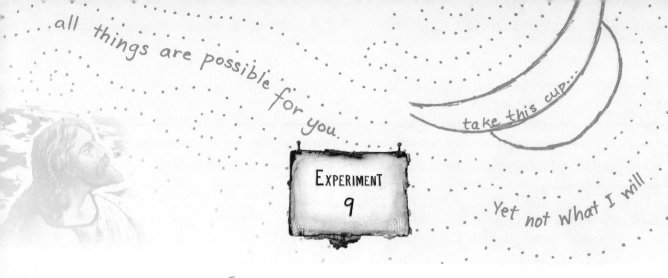

all things are possible for you...

take this cup...

Yet not what I will...

The (Other) Lord's Prayer

"Take this cup from me."
—MARK 14:36

The Themes: *prayer, faith, patience, Easter, Jesus*
The Reading: *Mark 14:32-39*

THE THINKING

I really, REALLY want something. Really. I've been wanting it for eight years. And I've been praying for the Lord to have what he wants, all along still wanting what I want. We live with that tension of wanting things yet knowing that we don't really understand what is best for us. How shall we approach God? Shall we stomp and pout, like spoiled children, demanding he grant our desires? Or offer the prayers of the defeated, never expecting blessings because we believe our God is too miserly? **Perhaps there's a middle ground.**

Jesus wanted things. He wanted to avoid a long, painful, torturous death. And he told his Father so (Mark 14:36). We usually consider the Lord's Prayer as Jesus' model prayer, but why not also see what we can take from his, very different, Gethsemane prayer? The traditional Lord's Prayer is a multipurpose prayer—adoration, confession, supplication, etc.—and can be used each day. But the Gethsemane prayer is one we can use to petition in desperation, as Jesus did. There was no beating around the bush—Jesus' pain drove him to get right to the point.

Look at the three parts of Jesus' prayer and think about how we can use them:

1. **"Abba, Father, everything is possible for you."** What a way to start a prayer! We can begin with a reminder of who it is we're addressing. We're not filling out paperwork to submit to some faceless bureaucrat—this is our *Father*. This part of the prayer also reminds us that there is no question that God *can* do what we ask. Whether our need is a new bike or a visit to Neptune, we know he can provide anything.

2. **"Take this cup from me."** Here's where we, like Jesus, can present our heart's desire. He wasn't afraid to be honest and admit he wanted something. Five syllables never had so much significance.

3. **"Yet not what I will, but what you will."** This final statement perfectly balances the prayer, making it very brief, but satisfying. Through this prayer we've acknowledged who God is and what he can do. We've been honest about our desires. And now we can end by giving God the last word. We entrust the outcome to a well-meaning, all-powerful being who knows our desires.

> *"Jesus prays to his Father that the cup may pass from him, and his Father hears his prayer; for the cup of suffering will indeed pass from him—but only by his drinking it."*
> —*Dietrich Bonhoeffer,*
> The Cost of Discipleship

How did the Father answer Jesus' prayer? With **a big, fat no,** it would seem. But this prayer isn't a magic formula to get wishes granted—it's a way to voice our wishes and to reconcile them to God's. For Jesus, God's plan didn't involve removal of that cup in the way we would expect. The Father had even greater provisions in mind. And Jesus was able to trust the Father's plan because of his faith in the truths expressed in this simple prayer.

THE MAKING

In school, teachers used to make children write out lines as a form of punishment. The hope was that by spending time writing the line "I will not put worms in Kenneth's lunch box," we would find ourselves less inclined to put worms in Kenneth's lunch box. I don't know how effective it is as a disciplinary tool, but writing does have a value for learning. Since as far back as Greco-Roman and early Christian times, writing has been seen as a personal exercise, a method of meditation (Michel Foucault, *Ethics*). The process of thinking, then writing, then rereading, then writing some more allows the writer to turn a thought over and over. After several lines, our hands have memorized the shapes of the letters, and our minds are able to reflect on the ideas behind what we're writing.

RECIPE FOR A MESS

I have a tendency to approach God with a list of things I've done for him, sometimes even taking pride in the fact that I'm praying to him (as if it's for his benefit!), and so I've learned the discipline of just being in his presence, of sitting quietly and just accepting his love and grace without feeling I have to earn it. Old married couples can just exist together without speaking much and are able to soak up each other's company, and I try to be that comfortable with God's company.

—M. P.

Use these *materials*:

- journaling template (provided on page 93)
- pencil or pen
- colored pencils (optional)

For this experiment we'll be using the journaling template provided (make photocopies—you can enlarge it if you like). Take some time to consider your heart's greatest desire—your own "Take This Cup from Me" prayer. It may be something you'd like removed or something you'd like God to add to your life.

Begin by writing the first part of the prayer—"Abba, Father, everything is possible for you"—on the dotted lines in the top half of the template (avoiding the cup). This is a sky-like space to reflect the unlimited love and power of God. Continue writing this part of the prayer until you've filled the top part of the template. If certain words stand out to you, repeat or emphasize them as you write. Throughout this experiment, you may need to rotate the page to change directions as you write.

Now, following the dotted lines again, fill in the cup with your own heartfelt request. Again, repeat it until that section is filled, highlighting important words, if you like. Finally, complete the lower section of the template—a ground-like space, since this sentiment is the foundation of every prayer—filling in the area around the base of the cup by repeatedly writing the final part of the prayer: "Yet not what I will, but what you will."

MAKING IT WORK FOR SMALL GROUPS OR CORPORATE WORSHIP SETTINGS

Decide if you want individuals to focus on their own prayers or to create a prayer as a group. Say the parts of the prayer together, stopping for reflection or journaling during the second part so that individuals can personalize the prayer with their own requests.

THE MEETING

1. Did the reminder of your relationship with God and his ability to do all things help? If so, how?

2. Do you regularly tell God what you want, even if it's not pretty? Or does it feel strange to be honest about your deepest desires? After doing this exercise, do you feel more able to leave your requests with him and trust him to answer with whatever is best?

3. How can you trust that, even if he doesn't answer in the way you wanted, he has other plans for you—that he will remove the cup in a different way than you expect?

4. Did the sky and ground elements of the journaling add anything to your interpretation? How so?

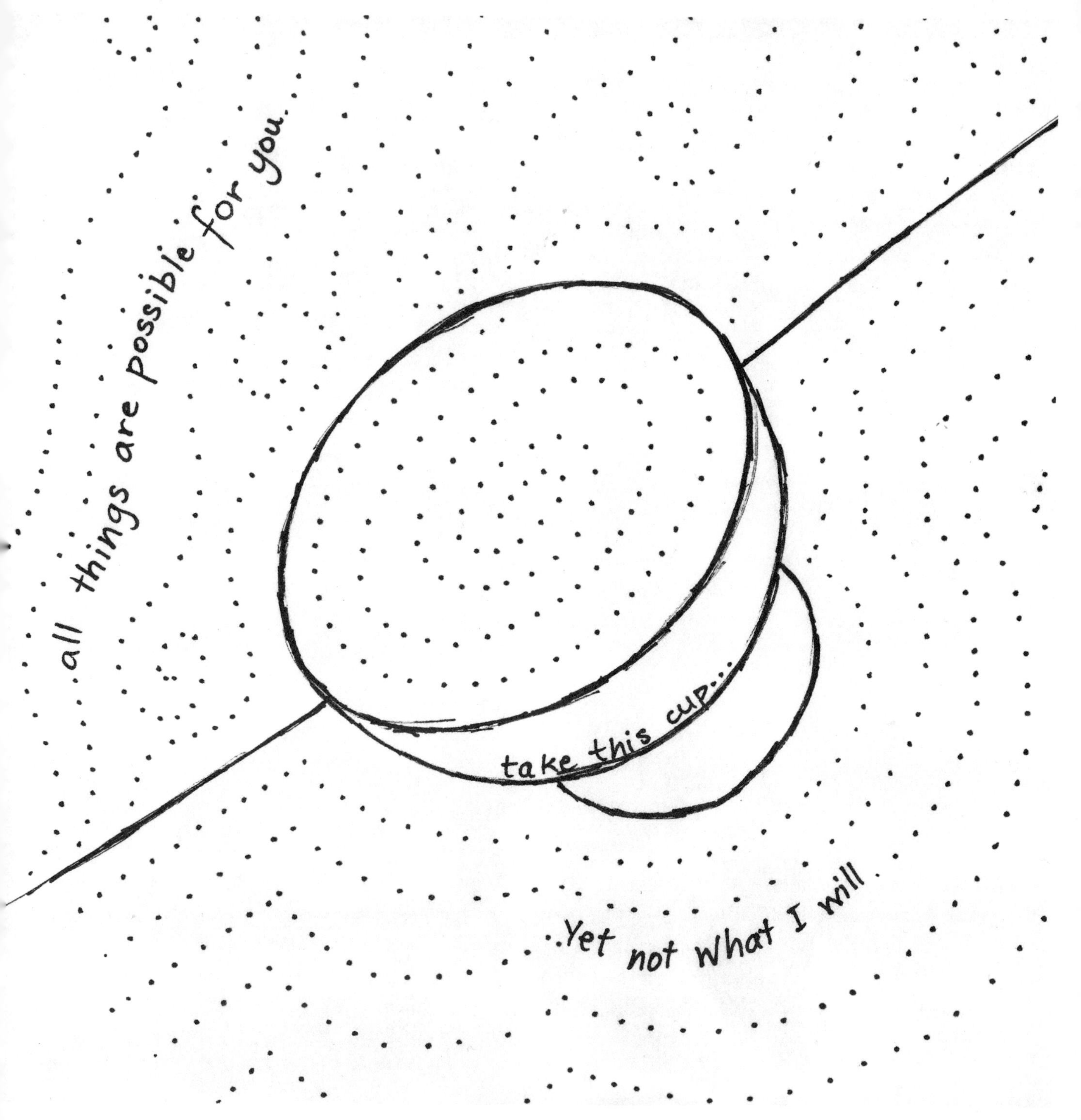
all things are possible for you.
take this cup...
Yet not what I will

Mixed Emotions

"There is a time for everything, and a season for every activity under heaven: . . .
a time to weep and a time to laugh, a time to mourn and a time to dance."
—ECCLESIASTES 3:1, 3

The Themes: emotion, color, balance
The Reading: Ecclesiastes 3:1-11

THE THINKING

My daughter and I are bored with hardware stores, but our eyes light up when we get to the paint-chip section. It's like shopping for colors. And while paint might have a price tag, at the hardware store they give away color for free! So each trip there sees us coming home with a new collection of paint chips. ("I would like a house that's Sonata Blue with a Dusky Evening fence!" "Oh yes, and I think this Tahiti Sunrise peach would go perfectly with your Listening to Rachmaninoff over Coffee on the Balcony beige.")

After a recent hardware store color hunt I read about the way Expressionist painters used color to express emotion and reflected on how naturally color evokes emotion in the human heart. Wouldn't it have been helpful if the Expressionists had had an authoritative color emotion guide they could turn to? "I want to express estrangement. Let's see . . . ahhh, yes, Alienation Gray would be perfect. Maybe with a touch of Self-Doubt Ochre."

So I created Mixed Emotions, a collection of my own color charts, labeling each color with what seemed to be the appropriate emotion. I was surprised at how much these paintings got people talking (here's where I have to admit that I visited the coffee shops where my paintings were exhibited and listened in on nearby conversations). "Oh no, that color's not Doubtful at all. It's too yellow to be doubtful. It's more hopeful, don't you think?"

The unexpected responses continued after the artwork was on a wall in my own home. After a friend house-sat for us, she confessed to me, "I love all your artwork but I have to say I'm a little disturbed by one piece." When she described the piece, I knew it was the color chart I called *The Neutrals*, which shows blocks of neutral colors paired with words for neutral emotions such as underwhelmed, detached, and listless. I didn't actually have all these feelings while I was painting this chart—this was just an experiment in how color evokes emotion—but my friend's comments made me see how much followers of Christ are often uncomfortable with strong or negative emotions.

Popular Christian music is often light and sentimental, and popular Christian art regularly depicts images of mountains or hands praying, or some combination of angels and children (on mountains with hands praying). I know that the composers and artists want to use their art to encourage and uplift, but do they inadvertently communicate "Nice Christians don't experience anger or depression or passion" or "If you trusted God enough, you wouldn't feel fear"? And maybe we've even come to believe in a warm, fuzzy deity who only feels warm, fuzzy feelings?

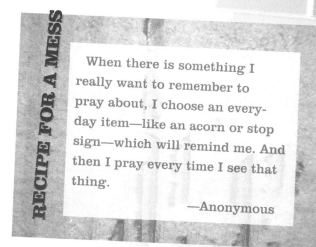

RECIPE FOR A MESS

When there is something I really want to remember to pray about, I choose an everyday item—like an acorn or stop sign—which will remind me. And then I pray every time I see that thing.

—Anonymous

Gloomy   Elated   Confused   Undecided   Furious

In Scripture, we see that David, Jesus, Paul, and the Father himself had no problem expressing strong emotions, both positive and negative. Just one day in Jesus' life is enough to provide an example. If you piece together the various Gospel accounts of the day of Jesus' triumphal entry, you see that it was an emotional roller-coaster ride for Jesus. Over the course of this single day, his hunger-induced frustration with a fig tree drives him to curse it, he is swept up in a joyful street party, he's caught off guard by a moment of mourning for the city, and explodes in righteous anger at the sight of greed in God's own temple (Matthew 21:1-16; Mark 11:1-17; Luke 19:28-45; John 2:12-17). The Gospel writers describe him as consumed with passionate emotion. And to top off this intense day, his ears are undoubtedly beginning to hear the whispers of a plot to kill him. Jesus was not a cardboard cutout with a permanent smile plastered on his face. He was immersed in this troubling, exciting, frustrating world, and he had no problem with feeling, and showing, all the emotion that this world evokes.

While not all of the strong emotions we feel are helpful or healthy, in order to deal with them we must first name them. And this is the point of this experiment, not to revel in our emotions for the sake of it, but to freely express them in order to process them and grow.

THE MAKING

Collect these materials:

- stretched canvas, canvas board, or thick cardboard
- pencil, eraser, ruler
- paintbrushes and/or wooden block
- fine-point permanent marker
- thesaurus (optional)
- assortment of acrylic paints

> "Color, like music, takes a shortcut to our senses and our emotions."
>
> —Philip Ball, *Bright Earth: Art and the Invention of Color*

Happy Excited Hungry Amazed Lonely Hopeful

My paintings describe emotions in general, however, the idea could be adapted to express how you feel toward God (curious, awed, grateful) or even to assign colors to various descriptions of God (majestic, present, caring). But it could just be a colorful journal entry, a visual inventory of how you feel on any given day (perhaps choose a color for how you're praying for people you care about—worried, rejoicing—and name the colors after them). It's just a way of showing God your feelings instead of telling him.

Decide how many emotions/descriptions you would like to paint (it might help to consult a thesaurus to gather emotion words) and divide up your canvas appropriately so that you have a small rectangle for each emotion. If you want to give the effect of a paint company's sample chart, line up the rectangles in rows with a little white space in between. Either fill in the rectangles with a paintbrush or use a rectangular block (e.g., a rectangular sponge or wooden block or find an uncut piece of rubber stamp in a craft supply store) to print the paint in a straight-edged shape.

After the paint has dried, with a fine-point marker carefully write the appropriate emotions/descriptions under each color. You can choose the emotions ahead and mix colors that suit them or just choose colors and find emotions to go with them after they're dry.

An adaptation: Choose colors for the emotions described or expressed in these Scripture passages. Label each color with Scripture quotes instead of emotions.

- Lamentations 1:16, 17
- Isaiah 55:12
- Ezekiel 36:6, 7
- Luke 19:37, 38
- Psalm 22:14-17
- Job 3:3-5

THE MEETING

1. How did it feel to acknowledge your emotions, especially those which may not be pleasant or which you may have felt guilty for feeling?

2. How did it feel to read passages of Scripture where people felt anger, shame, anxiety, and mourning? Were you able to find more positive emotions that had been obscured by the negative?

3. How can you express your negative emotions in a healthy, loving way? Did doing this experiment help you become more aware of your feelings about specific situations? What can you do with this awareness?

MAKING IT WORK FOR SMALL GROUPS OR CORPORATE WORSHIP SETTINGS

To create a simpler/quicker group exercise, collect an assortment of paint chips from hardware stores and remove the color labels. Provide pens, sheets of paper, and glue for individuals to create and label their own charts with the paint chips. If you want the group to complete an experiment as a whole, provide a large board with the colors already painted on it and, during a time of reflection, invite the group to label the colors as they see fit. Since this will mean each color gets many names, invite them to write on and around each color block. This can allow a group to process the emotions expressed in a biblical story, such as the Christmas or Easter story, creating such color names as "Magi Magenta" and "Crown of Thorns Green."

Or another way to link the emotion exercise with Scripture would be to put a portion of a Bible verse or verses on a board (either from a section your group is studying or just a verse you think would be helpful for this exercise) and let your group color (with crayons, markers, oil pastels, paint, or whatever is easiest) the space in and around or below the words with colors that represent the feelings those words give them. Then talk about why people associated certain colors with the words in the way that they did. For example, you could write a verse out in segments and let people color under each block of words:

TAKING IT TO THE STREET

Take the unlabeled paint chips or the rectangles of painted colors to a busy public place and ask passersby what emotion is expressed by each color. Record your findings.

Or create a large paint chart and take it to a park or shopping center and provide pens to allow the community to label the colors. Be sure to make signs explaining the project. Ask participants to keep it family-friendly.

Take photos of blocks of color in the streets around you—a yellow awning, a purple umbrella. Print the photos, arrange like a color chart or cut into triangles to make a color wheel, and label with the names of the places. You might be able to exhibit this work in a local coffee shop, library, restaurant, or other establishment. (See an example of this kind of piece on page 97.)

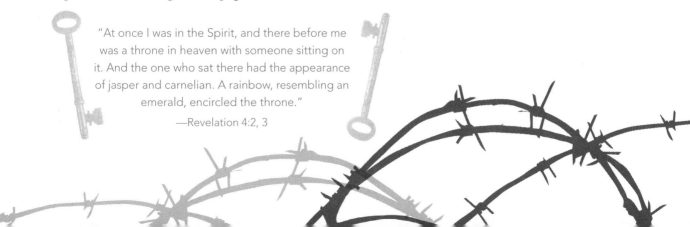

"At once I was in the Spirit, and there before me was a throne in heaven with someone sitting on it. And the one who sat there had the appearance of jasper and carnelian. A rainbow, resembling an emerald, encircled the throne."

—Revelation 4:2, 3

Elements of Making and Meeting

LESS IS MORE

"Eat what is good, and your soul will delight in the richest of fare."
—ISAIAH 55:2

When it comes to getting close to God, we've got it all wrapped up in the simple phrase **QUIET TIME**. But who invented it? And how are we supposed to get close to God in an age when we rarely have quiet and never have time? When I visited a major online Christian bookstore, I knew I wasn't the only one asking this question. A sidebar on the devotionals page asked, "Not Enough Time?" and offered a list of solutions, starting with Bible studies which take **ONE** minute a day!

I don't want to put off those readers for whom the traditional daily quiet time works, but I would like to challenge our usual mind–set about it to encourage those for whom it doesn't work, those for whom the Bible has become a big, dusty guilt-trip. There's no doubt that it's important to read it, but even the Bible itself doesn't tell us how or when. Paul never wrote "Read your Bible every morning for fifteen minutes" or "Memorize ten verses every week." But Scripture does say things like "Let the word of Christ dwell in you richly" (Colossians 3:16) and "I have hidden your word in my heart, that I might not sin against you" (Psalm 119:11).

How can we hide God's Word in our hearts, allow Christ's Word to dwell in us richly? Of the people I know, it seems prayer is a much easier way to make God a part of their lives. Even people who don't call themselves believers often pray. Somehow, it's easier to talk to God than to read the Bible every day. Perhaps we like to talk a lot more than we like to listen? But there are other things we can learn from the comparison of prayer and Bible reading.

"He who began a good work in you will carry it on to completion until the day of Christ Jesus." —Philippians 1:6

My husband and I have made a commitment to pray together every night. And to be honest, very rarely is it a time of spiritual invigoration. More often, the one praying takes a long pause, more from somnolence than solemnity. And more often, the one "listening" doesn't even notice! But this prayer routine is a way of officially ending the day, acknowledging God's part in it and handing to him all concerns before we go to sleep (well, before we *lie down* to go to sleep, anyway!). On the other hand, there are the heartfelt prayers that flow naturally during my days—the fervent pleading for help when I feel powerless, the awestruck praise when his goodness overwhelms me, and even the angry questions in the midst of calamity. These prayers have little in common with our bedtime recitations. And yet, both are prayer and both are necessary.

So what does this have to do with reading the Bible? While many times, reading takes discipline, there have been other times when a Bible reading has gone STRAIGHT TO MY SOUL. Like the time the words "Joy comes in the morning" came to me from nowhere with each contraction as I gave birth to my daughter. In the midst of all the postnatal fuss, I couldn't rest until I'd tracked down that verse and read it in context. There was the time a friend had questions about a particular doctrine and I became a search engine, flipping pages to cross-reference passages and work out what I believed about the whole thing. Another time I read the book of Ecclesiastes in one sitting, soaking up every word as if my life depended upon it. But these moments are few and far between.

For me, there are (at least) two kinds of devotional Bible reading, both important in the Christian walk. There's the regular reading which, like regular prayer times, may become dull and routine. Then there are the inspiring moments in the Word, like those prayers which are meaningful and spontaneous. Daily readings and prayer are like a regular intake of fiber in a daily diet—sometimes dry but always essential. A diet is balanced when we have bran flakes every morning and only expect a steak dinner with a chocolate sundae every now and then. The same is true with our spiritual diet.

It's OK to crave "steak." God is honored that we want to know his truth more and dig our teeth into something meaty. But here's the problem: when we believe that spiritual growth equals reading ten minutes of the Bible every morning or fifteen verses every night, and then when that ten minutes or those fifteen verses don't do much for us, we think it's the Bible's fault and give up. Yet, we believe the Bible is powerful, and we may even have had some powerful experiences with its truths. So we have to wonder, if we're honest, why do we rarely feel that power? Perhaps we're in such a hurry, tallying our verses or counting the minutes, that we miss it.

RECIPE FOR A MESS

I put Post-it notes everywhere. I mean everywhere, from the head of my bed, to my bathroom mirror, and the kitchen cabinets. The Post-it notes are of various Scriptures that I have read in daily devotions. It helps me retain his teachings and reinforce them in my psyche.

—P. D.

Truth is a heavy reality and it takes time to soak into our brains, which are already heavily saturated with things that are not Truth.

Since we have very little scriptural advice on when and how to read the Bible, I'm just going to tell you what I think: Slow down. Choose one, small, meaningful passage and read it every day until you get it. Put it on your refrigerator and in your calendar and just live with it throughout your day. It will collide with the realities of the world and show you the many facets of truth it holds. You might find that after a while, what you thought was dry bran starts to take on new flavor. After all, steak takes some chewing! So as we develop spiritually, we must count our growth in terms of quality and depth, not in a tally of verses read, prayers said, or services attended. Having a relationship with God is not about working our way to him but about working out how to discover that he's already there.

TAKE A MOMENT

1. Stop and think about your assumptions about quiet time and the spiritual discipline of reading Scripture. What goals have you set for yourself in terms of number of verses read or amount of time in prayer? Where did you get these assumptions and goals? Are they scriptural? How do you feel when you don't meet your goal? Are those feelings valid?

2. What have you found meaningful in your Bible reading/study? What is more of a challenge? In what ways can you incorporate more of the meaningful kinds of Bible study?

3. Choose one brief (ten verses or less) Bible passage to live with for a week. As you use it, notice whether you get tired of it or if you find yourself noticing something new each time. Read it in different places, with different music playing, in different ways (use a variety of translations, read it aloud, write it out, listen to an audio version). Make notes each day of what is meaningful to you from the passage. By the end of the week you will have a multifaceted reading of it. What truths stayed with you from the verse or verses? Would singing a Psalm or listening to an audio Bible or discussing Scripture with a friend also count as ways to "let the word of Christ dwell" in us richly? If so, what other ways might count? (For some creative ideas, check out a Web site set up by the American Bible Society, www.engage.american bible.org, where you can sign up to have a minute of Scripture sent to your cell phone, download audio Bible passages, and more. You can also check out the resources offered at www.biblegateway.com.)

"I have quitted all forms of devotion and set prayers but those to which my state obliges me. And I make it my business only to persevere in His holy presence, wherein I keep myself by a simple attention, and a general fond regard of God, which I may call an actual presence of God."

—Brother Lawrence,
The Brother Lawrence Collection

Elements of Making and Meeting

THE SPECIALNESS
OF THE ORDINARY

*"God did this so that men would seek him and perhaps reach out
for him and find him, though he is not far from each one of us.
'For in him we live and move and have our being.'"*
—Acts 17:27, 28

A t a recent conference, a well-known Christian speaker and writer challenged the traditional view of quiet time. She made the thought-provoking statement that all of life is spiritual formation, not only the times we call quiet time. Many in the audience nodded in agreement, and I agreed it was a timely message. However, when she started to give examples, she told about once-in-a-lifetime experiences that had drawn her close to God. Undoubtedly, God makes himself known to us in mountaintop experiences, and these are often moments we cling to at times of spiritual dryness and doubt. I certainly have some stories of my own which involve God revealing his goodness through shooting stars and empty beaches and towering trees.

But I have a problem with these moments. Two, actually. One is that we have no control over them. They often arrive uninvited. In fact, their unexpectedness is part of the awe they inspire. My other problem is that these moments don't usually happen in the middle of our ordinary life. It's often the unusual nature of our setting or activity which draws us out of our routine enough to notice God's presence. In other words, if we tried to live on the mountaintop, soon the endless view would lose its power (and the boss would wonder where we were). So, while I agree that all of life is spiritual formation, it must be found somehow in the ordinary tasks of our daily work and communities and families. As Dallas Willard put it in his book *The Divine Conspiracy*, "The obviously well kept secret of the 'ordinary' is that it is made to be a receptacle of the divine, a place where the life of God flows. But the divine is not pushy."

How can we stop and notice that quiet divine which waits under every leaf, in the face of every child, and at every stoplight?

"Fix these words of mine in your hearts and minds; tie them as symbols on your hands and bind them on your foreheads. Teach them to your children, talking about them when you sit at home and when you walk along the road, when you lie down and when you get up. Write them on the doorframes of your houses and on your gates."
—Deuteronomy 11:18-20

"Our actions should unite us with God when we are involved in our daily activities, just as our prayer unites us with Him in our quiet time."

—Brother Lawrence,
The Brother Lawrence Collection

"Heaven and earth are full of thy glory." —Book of Common Prayer

TAKE A MOMENT

1. Are there ordinary parts of your day which have a spiritual significance for you? What are they? How do you connect to God through them?

2. When taking part in an everyday activity, ask yourself how this could be an opportunity for connection with God. Without changing the task, can it become a spiritual activity simply by changing our approach and mind–set? Is there an opportunity to see God, or to be thankful, or to ask for help—one that you have missed before? Take apart your daily routines. What kind of spiritual potential could you find in driving or filing or shaving or walking?

3. What does "quiet time" mean for you?

"I am who I am." —Exodus 3:14

Who I Am

The Themes: humility. God's sovereignty. partnership with God. servanthood. faith. guidance. balance

The Reading: Exodus 3

THE THINKING

Writing a résumé for a ministry position requires a tricky balance. Anyone teaching a seminar on résumé writing will tell you to sell your good points and do all you can to make the search committee ask, "Where have you been all our lives?!" But a ministry résumé requires the applicant to subtly list their skills, experience, honors, and awards, all the while seeming humble and willing to give God the credit.

When we do God's work (which, of course, all Christians do in one way or another), where do we find the line between what *we* do and what *God* does? Is it about the gifts he has given me or about my ability to trust him to provide the skills? Is it about my working to set and accomplish goals or about listening for and following his lead? Of course, the answer is yes.

When I started in my current ministry, I struggled with these questions, at times jumping in with both feet and, only after several weeks of brainstorming and planning, asking God to bless my work. At other times, I timidly hesitated to make a move, out of doubt in my own ability and concern that I might step on God's toes. In an e-mail to a friend I confessed, "I'm finding it such a challenge to balance feeling so good about my own ability that I don't trust God and feeling so bad about my own ability that I don't trust God (if that makes any sense)!"

Soon after writing this e-mail, I read through Exodus 3. As I did, I underlined all the uses of the word *I*. Try it yourself, if you like. Here's what I learned: As God and Moses talk about the situation of God's people in Egypt, God uses *I* to tell Moses how things will be done and Moses uses *I* to tell God all the ways his plan is impossible. God makes these powerful statements: "*I* have seen the misery of my people. . . . *I* have heard . . . *I* am concerned. . . . *I* have come down. . . . *I* am sending you." And after all of that, Moses' little voice squeaks, "Who am *I*?" So God confidently replies, "*I* will be with you. . . . it is *I* who have sent you." To which Moses whimpers, "Suppose *I* go, who shall *I* say has sent me?" And God ends the conversation in the simplest and yet most baffling way: "I AM."

Like Moses, we ask God how we can do his work and hope he will encourage us by reminding us of our strengths. But instead he turns us to his own.

Slowly I'm learning now to look for a balance, to work in partnership with an invisible force, to speak with my ears always open, to expect detours in my plans. I'm learning to see that although the word sounds the same, *I* means something very different when God says it. It's an ongoing lesson, but gradually it's getting easier to remember who I am and to remember "I AM."

THE MAKING

Scavenge for these materials:

* paper in a variety of colors/patterns (For example, origami papers in a variety of colors/textures/patterns are often sold in packs in craft/art stores. Card-making and scrapbooking departments of craft stores also often sell interesting selections of papers. Or dump out your paper

recycling bin.) If you have time, make the patterns yourself on the paper with paint (finger-paint or flick the paint with a toothbrush or, while the paint is still wet, make patterns or scribbles in it with the end of the paintbrush) or colored pencils (scribble is fine).

- tracing paper or vellum paper (partly transparent paper available in art stores and scrapbook sections of craft stores)
- magazines (optional)
- pencils/fine-point markers
- scissors
- tape
- glue sticks

Choose two of the colored/patterned/painted pieces of paper, one that represents your mood when you feel unworthy and incapable and the other representing how you feel when you have great confidence in your own worth and abilities. Tape these side by side to form one sheet with two very different halves and, with a marker, label the first Who Am I? (for the times, like Moses, that we doubt ourselves) and the second Who I Am (for the times we're puffed up with our own self-importance).

Choose words to write or cut words and phrases from magazines to paste on these pages in the appropriate places. If you're using a magazine, rather than looking for particular words, let the available words guide you. For the Who Am I? side, you might find the words *empty*, *nothing special* and *uncertain*, and on the Who I Am page, you might choose *clever*, *Bravo!* and *efficient*. If additional words come to mind, add them to the mix in handwriting.

I Am Poem

I am _frightened._
I wonder _what these people are thinking._
I hear _people shouting at me._
I see _soldiers beside me._
I want _this to end._
I am _being crucified._
I pretend _I am already in heaven._
I feel _blood and sweat on my face._
I touch _this painful cross._
I worry _that my mom is weeping with sadness_
I cry _out for help._
I am _so worried_
I understand _I have to die._
I say _"Father, forgive these people."_
I dream _I am not here._
I try _to understand people who hate me._
I hope _that I can make it through._
I am _brave because my father is with me_

—Colette O'Regan,
"I Am Poem," *Voices*

Teachers often give their students the exercise of writing "I Am" poems. Each line begins with *I* and a verb, and the children finish the sentences. This "I Am" poem was written, from Jesus' perspective, by a nine-year-old. I include it here because it portrays that delicate balance between his own fear and his faith. Follow this format and try writing your own "I Am" poems, one for when you doubt your own ability, one for when you're overly confident in your own ability, and one from God's perspective.

Take a piece of tracing paper or vellum (or other translucent material) that is large enough to overlap both of these sides. Lay it over them and tape or glue the top edge of the vellum to the top of the two side-by-side sheets in such a way so the vellum can be lifted up. Label the piece of tracing paper or vellum with I AM. Around the words *I AM* paste words which reflect God's nature and/or your relationship with him, such as *leaning on him, my God, open to possibilities, his name*. You will be able to see through the vellum to read parts of the two underlying extremes. The upper layer with words about God will remind us that, regardless of how competent we think we are, or aren't, God's competence is over all, just as God's use of *I* covered all of Moses' uses of the word.

MAKING IT WORK FOR SMALL GROUPS OR CORPORATE WORSHIP SETTINGS

When using this experiment for a group, it may help to cut a selection of words/phrases from magazines ahead of time rather than offer whole magazines—flipping through pages may distract from the project. Choose adjectives that could be used to describe individuals or God, and words that could relate to faith (for example: *listen, I felt it was God's hand, leaning, learn, trust*).

As with all group projects, decide if you'd like individuals to experiment alone but at the same time or if the group will create a large project together.

THE MEETING

1. Do you ever struggle with finding a balance between feeling so good about your own ability that you don't trust God and feeling so bad about your own ability that you don't trust God? In what situations?

2. Describe a time you should have had more faith in the gifts God had given you and a time you should have had less faith in your own abilities. How could your reliance on him depend more on who he is than on who you are?

3. How does the placement of the sheet about God affect the words you chose about yourself? How are the words about him related to the words about you?

"And he who searches our hearts
knows the mind of the Spirit."
—ROMANS 8:27

EXPERIMENT
12

Life as Lectio

The Themes: prayer, contemplation, patience, distraction, focus
The Reading: Romans 8

THE THINKING

Like all Christ followers, I have learned that prayer is a discipline. It takes work. When it's hard, you just keep trying. But without meaning to, this approach can create a works mentality, an I-can-only-commune-with-God-if-I-focus-hard-enough-for-long-enough work ethic. There's no room in that philosophy for bad days (or weeks) or mental exhaustion or, heaven forbid, God's great patience and ability to wrangle meaning from our feeble moans. The times in my life when I have most needed to pray are also the times in my life when I have been most unable to pray, either from being overwhelmed by my emotions, by my environment, or by fatigue. If we go by what Romans 8:26, 27 has to say, we will remember that God has more patience and understands more than we give him credit for: "In the same way, the Spirit helps us in our weakness. We do not know what we ought to pray for, but the Spirit himself intercedes for us with groans that words cannot express. And he who searches our hearts knows the mind of the Spirit, because the Spirit intercedes for the saints in accordance with God's will."

Lectio divina is a way of reading Scripture which involves *patience and understanding*. The same passage of Scripture is read several times and it's often not until the third time that it starts to sink in. So I've learned to apply those *lectio* lessons of patience and understanding to my prayers.

I live in a neighborhood that has more than its fair share of challenges and so, when I decided to wake early in the morning every Sunday to go for an hour-long prayer walk, I was at a loss to know how to do that safely. I felt safe, alone and in the dark, only within a small area, so I decided to walk a loop of that area three times. When I started these walks, with my first step out the door, I forced my mind to begin praying. But my mind wandered. Eventually, rather than make my sleepy head perform, I *embraced the wandering.*

I began to see my first loop as a chance to take the lid off a very full jar and let the contents spill out in whatever order they liked. The issues that were mundane—How should I respond to that e-mail? What should I get my son for his birthday?—often presented themselves first. By the second loop I began to see recurring themes in my thoughts and concerns. It was fascinating to notice how at the same corner at which, on the first loop, I had worried about a friend's health, her face came to mind again on the the second time around. But by then I was closer to being able to put my thoughts into prayers. And I also discovered that things I saw reminded me of various people and the prayers they needed—at one point I can see my children's school; at another I can see the steeple of a church whose pastor is ill.

During the last loop I began to form the first drafts of a prayer. People say that walking aids digestion. I've found this true for both food and thoughts. By my third loop, my mind was cleared of distractions; *my prayers were ready to be expressed.* And God was good enough, in this troubled neighborhood, to place a hilltop. I finished my walk overlooking the whole city—a grand vista always makes anything seem possible—and finally could speak my prayers to him. One hour of walking for five minutes of heartfelt, focused prayer.

THE MAKING

Try these steps:

- Find a circuit to walk and ease into the prayer as you go.
- If you like, designate places to reflect on various prayer concerns and pray about them each time you pass. Note how the prayers evolve with each loop.
- Choose a stopping point at the end of your circuit—preferably a place with some quiet or natural beauty—to pray a prayer that sums up all the issues that arose while walking.
- Print a map of the places you walked (www.googlemaps.com) to write in the prayers you prayed.

RECIPE FOR A MESS

I ride my bike across the bridge to Covington several days a week for work. I have made it a habit to stop in the middle of the bridge (on the pedestrian sidewalk) to admire the beauty of the Ohio River and the view of the cities. I dedicate the moment to God by praying the Lord's Prayer and then ride on.
—A. U.

MAKING IT WORK FOR SMALL GROUPS OR CORPORATE WORSHIP SETTINGS

Print a large map of the neighborhood/city. Give each person a different colored marker or highlighter and ask them to trace the routes they walk/drive every day. How can they make those circuits opportunities for prayer? Are there points along the way that they can designate as places to pray for particular people/concerns?

Walk a prayer circuit (of the neighborhood or church grounds/building) in silence as a group, stopping along the way to record, on printed maps, phrases or people that come to mind. Finish by praying as a group.

> "Healthy prayer necessitates frequent experiences of the common, earthly, run-of-the-mill variety. Like walks, and talks, and good wholesome laughter. . . . To be spiritually fit to scale the Himalayas of the spirit, we need regular exercise in the hills and valleys of ordinary life."
>
> —Richard Foster,
> *Prayer: Finding the Heart's True Home*

THE MEETING

1. How did you feel about praying at the beginning of your walk? Did your attitude toward prayer change at all by the end of your walk? If so, how?

2. As you looped past familiar spots, how did your thoughts begin to track with your environment?

3. Were you able to uncover important issues hidden under the mundane? What were they? How are mundane thoughts sometimes connected to deeper, significant ones?

4. What have you found that helps you most to clear your mind and pray with more focus? Have you tried other such experiments besides walking? What were they? What worked well? What didn't?

TAKING IT TO THE STREET

Make a prayer circuit a weekly or monthly part of the life of your church. Invite the neighbors to join in—ask them to walk with you or just ask them if they have anything they would like you to pray about.

If you and your fellow prayer walkers are especially Web savvy, you could even make your own customized prayer walk maps by using the My Maps function on Google Maps. This feature allows you to add photos and text to a map route that you create, and then you can share this map with others.

Elements of Making and Meeting

SOCIAL BEINGS (AND DOINGS)

"Now you are the body of Christ, and each one of you is a part of it."
—1 CORINTHIANS 12:27

"Immortal, Invisible, God Only Wise/ In Light inaccessible, hid from our eyes. . . ." moved nicely into: "We bow down,/ We lay our crowns at the feet of Jesus."

Together we were talking to him.

Then the drums kicked in, the tempo surged and these words popped up on the screen: "Over the mountains and the sea,/ Your river runs with love for me./ And I will open up my heart/ And let the healer set me free."

Like a magic spell, the switch of pronouns turned everyone else invisible. The contrast was so real, I almost heard a click as we switched channels from a group of people, together acknowledging each other and their God, to a bunch of individuals with blinders on. Or maybe the blinders are more like a blindfold—not only blocking those around us but also blocking out God so that our own experiences and feelings are the focus

"Since you are eager to have spiritual gifts, try to excel in gifts that build up the church."

—1 Corinthians 14:12

of our worship. Worship songs are often written during times of intense personal conviction, then sung by large groups. But their inward, individual focus remains.

All this has been said before, but I felt I had to leave you with a little caution. Worship through art and experimentation also can have a way of blindfolding us. We ourselves become the work of art that we constantly assess, tweak, create, to present the world with a masterpiece. Experimentation, especially when our own spirits, minds, and emotions are drawn into the experiment, can feel like navel-gazing.

These experiments are certainly usable in group worship (as a family/small group/at a retreat), however, even if you use these in a private worship setting, they are to be used still with the community, the church, and the world in mind. The point here is to take some time out alone, not only for personal gain (although that may certainly be a by-product), but so that you can develop and process an idea, a feeling, a belief, in order to better use it, live it, share it in the home, workplace, school, community, and congregation.

RECIPE FOR A MESS

There are few moments when God is more obviously present for me than when people make noise together. To hear the collective sounds of human voices raised to God and to join in, I'm somehow lost in the sound.

—A. S.

Yes, experimentation can be a gift to God, but it is meaningful to him because it is a promise of action. These experiments, and the lessons they hold, aren't the end, but the beginning of the process.

TAKE A M⊙MENT

1. Think back to a time when you were part of a large group of people doing something together, whether it was singing in a choir or doing the wave at a sports event. How did it feel? Did you feel lost in the crowd or did you feel somehow greater by being part of something bigger than yourself?

2. Do you ever, in the midst of your normal life, get a sense that you are part of something bigger than yourself? If not, what could you do to get that sense?

3. Can you recite the Lord's Prayer? Or write it out? We often focus on the daily bread, the forgiveness, the temptation, and skip over the pronouns. Write out the prayer (from Matthew 6:9-13), taking note of and highlighting the pronouns. Does the one praying use singular or plural pronouns for him/herself? Pray the prayer using "I," then using "we." What difference does it make?

"Art promotes community integration and interaction. Music, dance, and painting, so often part of harvest festivals and religious observances, bring people together to 'sing with one voice.' Art is part of a deep, preverbal communication that binds people together. It is literally a communion."

—Stuart Brown with Christopher Vaughan, *Play: How It Shapes the Brain, Opens the Imagination, and Invigorates the Soul*

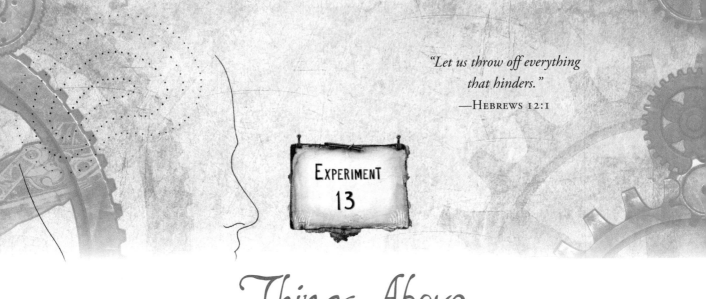

EXPERIMENT
13

Things Above

The Themes: spirituality. worldliness. Heaven

The Reading: Colossians 3:1-17; Philippians 4:8. 9; Hebrews 12:1-3

THE THINKING

Today I took the dog for a walk, as I always do, in the same places where we always walk. Our route takes us past a spot, on the top of a grassy hill, where I swear the sky is bigger than anywhere else between here and "Big Sky Country." But it wasn't until I ducked inside my doorway that I looked back and beheld the huge, pink sun I had been walking under. An immense, fuschia ball of burning gas had been hovering over my head and I had been blind to it. But there was nothing wrong with my eyes. This was a brain blindness. As big as the sky had been and as bright as the sun had shone, this morning my eyes, and thoughts, were on the ground.

In Colossians 3:2, Paul writes, **"Set your minds on things above, not on earthly things."** But if I couldn't even literally set my mind on things above, how am I supposed to do it figuratively? It's not as simple as flipping channels. There is a **cloud of mental chatter**—concerns, ideas, memories—between us and "things above." Even to begin to remember that there are higher planes of thought, first we have to stop and clear that cloud. This creative journaling experiment will help us with that **first step.**

THE MAKING

You'll need:

- Copy of the journaling template (from page 121, enlarge if you like)
- Pens/pencils/colored pencils

Take a minute or two of silence and note the thoughts floating around in your head. Beginning at the outer edge of the brain shape and rotating the sheet as you go, write words which represent the issues that fill your mind—*dentist appointment, Mom's surgery, anniversary, roof repair, meeting Friday.*

This may be a good experiment to help prepare for other experiments or times of study, or it may be used to lead into a time of prayer or journaling.

MAKING IT WORK FOR SMALL GROUPS OR CORPORATE WORSHIP SETTINGS

For a group setting, make copies of the template. Enlarge them if you like. To create a very large version, scan this image and paste it into a digital slide program to project from a LCD projector or trace the image on an overhead transparency sheet. Project the image onto a large, flat surface (whiteboard or large sheet of paper) and follow the lines with a marker. Allow the group (perhaps during a time of reflection or during a worship set) to come to the image when they're ready and write a few things on it.

"Finally, brothers, whatever is true, whatever is noble, whatever is right, whatever is pure, whatever is lovely, whatever is admirable—if anything is excellent or praiseworthy—think about such things."
—Philippians 4:8

1. Were you surprised to find how much was filling your mind? What kinds of things were taking up your thoughts? Were they more trivial or significant?

2. Once you cleared away those thoughts, did you find that it was easier to focus on "things above"? What things from above were waiting for your attention?

RECIPE FOR A MESS

As children, we are taught to clear our minds and close our eyes and still our bodies before focusing on God. It's important to focus, especially when you're a squirmy kid, but after being taught that as a kid, I've spent the rest of my life trying to reconnect my spirit with my body and mind. The older I get, the more I understand that my mind, soul, and body are all interconnected. If I neglect my body, it affects my mind and soul and vice versa. How can I show love to people if I'm too sick or tired from ignoring my body's needs for exercise, rest, and good food? How can I focus on things above if I haven't ordered my mind? So when I take part in the physical and intellectual side of my life, I try to be conscious of how they are interwoven with my spiritual life. I ask myself things like: How does my choice of food support what I'm trying to do in my spiritual and intellectual life? How does the way I fill my mind support my physical and spiritual goals?

—Anonymous

3. What does setting your mind on things above mean to you? Does setting your mind on things above mean shutting this world out to some extent? Why or why not?

4. Go back to the mundane and "things below" issues you wrote in the journaling template. How can you see them as God sees them and set your mind on things above while looking at things below?

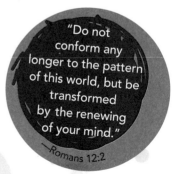

"Do not conform any longer to the pattern of this world, but be transformed by the renewing of your mind."
—Romans 12:2

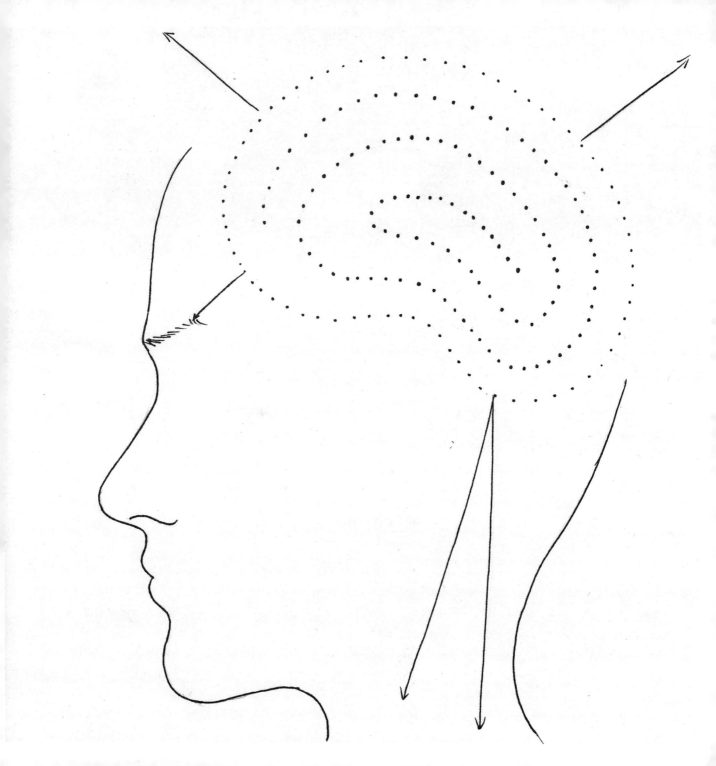

EXPERIMENT
14

The Rest Is Up to You

"You will find rest for your souls."
—MATTHEW 11:29

The Themes: Sabbath, rest, faith, stress, humility, stillness
The Reading: Exodus 20:8-11; Psalm 46; Matthew 11:28-30; Mark 2:23-28

THE THINKING

I had a totally snow-free childhood. Since I grew up in Australia, it wasn't until I moved to the United States at the age of eighteen that I discovered the joys of snow. And so, of course, until then I also had no idea what a snow day was—not a snowy day, a Snow Day. Snow, in itself, is magical enough. But when you and all your friends suddenly have nothing to do for the day and a playground of white has fallen from the sky, you have to wonder if you've been granted a piece of childhood. All the assignments are postponed; all the schedules are thrown out.

But responsible adults often forget the true spirit of the snow day. We're grown-ups now. Our time and work is very important. We find a way to get our work done, snow day or not. When our bodies say "I'm sick, let me rest!" we pop a few pills and keep on working. When our bodies say "I'm tired, let me rest!" we just take it as a sign to order the double espresso.

I've learned from living in other places, and from talking to internationals, how little our culture allows rest as a normal part of daily life. In some countries they have *siesta*—all the stores close in the afternoon and people—grown-ups!—take a nap for an hour or so. In other places they have a tea or coffee ritual—in Britain, many workplaces actually hire someone to fill the position of "The Tea Lady," a person (usually a lady) who takes tea and cookies around to all the employees every day at 10 and 2. In some countries, in order to create more jobs, employers give each employee a scheduled day off once a month. So rest becomes a normal part of the daily or monthly routine.

But our culture doesn't allow for rest. For many of us, rest is a big special thing that happens once a year on vacation, not a daily part of life. So we have to be very proactive, creative, even revolutionary, to break the cycle. This isn't about planning a special trip, about "getting away from it all"—that in itself is often work. We just need to learn how to drop what we're doing where we are, on ordinary days and in ordinary places.

I've been practicing this over the past year and it's harder than you'd think! I get the feeling it's hard for most of us. One day, in an effort to make rest a normal part of life, I stopped, on a workday, to have lunch. I was still trying to mentally set aside my to-do list and overcome my feelings of guilt for taking thirty minutes for myself when a coworker saw me with my Thai take-out and magazine and asked, "Oh, you don't have much on today?"

Stopping is just the beginning of celebrating the Sabbath through resting and delighting in God, but since it's so hard for us, we need to get used to this first step at least.

RECIPE FOR A MESS

In recent years I have become prone to waking up at night, and I have trouble getting back to sleep. I have turned this problem into an opportunity to spend time reading poetry and praying. The kind of intimacy with God that I find nearly impossible to achieve during the day, even during a quiet time, seems practically effortless during the stillness and isolation of the night. And eventually I get sleepy, and then my sleep is also restful.
—R. B.

THE MAKING

Experiment 14a

This experiment may be the simplest, yet most challenging, of all. It is to do nothing, to take five minutes of time—like a mini snow day—to daydream. For many of us, the Sunday sermon is the only time we sit still, and suddenly all the thoughts, feelings, and ideas of the week are able to be processed without the TV or Internet or other distractions. Imagine if we allowed ourselves time every day or every week to do that. How much more present would we be for our relationships with God and others? (Or for the sermon!)

Of course, you can spend the time praying if you like, but you don't have to pray in order to make this spiritual. This is an opportunity to discover that stopping, in itself, can be a spiritual thing. This is a time to practice being OK with doing nothing. Don't force yourself to be productive or to discipline your mind to think in a logical way. Perhaps you will remember it's your mom's birthday this month or maybe you'll work out why you've been feeling angry all week or you'll make a shopping list. Whether you learn how much your mind needed to sort your ideas and feelings, or you take the time to pray, or you spend the entire time fidgeting because you're uncomfortable with nothing to do, the exercise, hopefully, will show you how much you need time outside of normal time. Even daydreaming can be a spiritual thing when we do it with a consciousness of God's presence and with the goal of clearing our minds to be more whole and more aware. For an extra challenge, turn off all the lights, the TV, and the radio, and sit in the dark, without any external stimulation. Can you do it? For how long?

Experiment 14b

We regularly whine, "Why doesn't God speak directly to me?" But if he did, would we really want to listen? When I first heard of a free service to send a minute of the Bible to my cell phone, I signed up for an experimental month to receive a phone call every weekday at noon. This would both remind me to take a lunch break and help me start it with a reminder of God's presence. Just one minute of the Bible. Sounds great, right?

You would be surprised how often I wanted to let that call go straight to voicemail. People would look at me and ask, "Did you know your phone's ringing?" and I would joke, "Oh, it's just God." It made me see how much I'm not ready to drop what I'm doing, even if I know God is calling me. (To sign up for this free service, go to www.411God.net. See also www.faithcomesbyhearing.com for another audio Bible option and www.thedaily bibleverse.com to receive Bible passages through text messages, e-mail and Facebook. Set it up for a limited period of time—a week or a month—for this experiment so that you can assess whether or not to continue. If you decide to cancel the service, don't feel guilty—you're not actually rejecting God, just a phone service.)

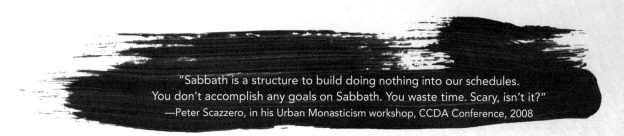

"Sabbath is a structure to build doing nothing into our schedules. You don't accomplish any goals on Sabbath. You waste time. Scary, isn't it?"
—Peter Scazzero, in his Urban Monasticism workshop, CCDA Conference, 2008

Experiment 14c

About five years ago my watch ran out of batteries and I didn't have time to get them replaced immediately. So I entered the scary world of not knowing the time. Wherever I went, I found myself scanning the walls for clocks, always fearing that maybe I was late for something. But after a while, I got used to it, even felt freed by it. I understood why, in *Gulliver's Travels*, the Lilliputians believe that Gulliver's watch is his God—he keeps it close and consults it before doing anything. So here's the experiment—simply take off your watch. Start with doing it for one day and see if you can stretch yourself to leaving it off for two days or even a week. Of course, you'll need to consult devices that tell time at points throughout the day and that's fine—every cell phone, computer, and microwave is happy to remind you of the seconds ticking by—but do you really need time strapped to your wrist?

MAKING IT WORK FOR SMALL GROUPS OR CORPORATE WORSHIP SETTINGS

Give your group the opportunity to have a mini snow day during your time together (with the introduction from Experiment 14a). Provide instrumental music, if you'd like (I've used a beautiful piece called *Sur Le Fil* by Yann Tiersen). Provide an opportunity afterwards for the group to discuss or journal about how they used the time, whether they were comfortable, what they learned from it (even if it was that they don't like having nothing to do).

THE MEETING

Experiment 14a

1. When you took time to stop, did it feel strange to have nothing to do? How long has it been since you had nothing to do?

2. What do you think would happen if you tried stopping for longer next time? Would it drive you crazy? Would it drive others crazy?

3. What did you think about when you were daydreaming? How could you work more space into your life to daydream and clear your mind on a regular basis?

Experiment 14b

1. If you tried this experiment, how did you feel about receiving the call (or the message, e-mail, etc.)? Were you ready to receive it or unwilling to stop what you were doing? Why?

2. If you took time regularly to rest, do you think you would be more open to unexpected, and inconvenient, promptings from God? Why or why not? What would help you to be more open to such experiences?

Experiment 14c

1. Was it scary to take off your watch? If so, what did you fear? Could you make it through the day without checking the time?

2. Would taking time for rest help break your reliance on knowing the time? Why or why not?

All experiments

1. Why do you think God instituted the idea of the Sabbath? Psalm 46:10 tells us to be still and know

> **"The great American vacation is slipping away. The number of Americans taking off from work for less than a full week at a time has more than doubled since 1990."**
> —Francis Wilkinson, Editorial, *The Week Magazine*, July 31, 2009

that God is God and Exodus 31:13 says we must observe Sabbaths so that we may know that he is God. What do you think is the connection between regular resting and knowing God?

2. How is faith a part of stopping? What will stopping teach us about ourselves? about God?

3. What would it look like for you to stop on a daily or weekly basis? How can you work stopping into your schedule/budget/family/work? Could it be going to bed an hour earlier once a week? Stopping for tea for fifteen minutes a day? Taking an extra long bath once a week? Ordinary things take on great significance when we do them with purpose and plan for them. Unlike the snow day, it needs to be planned but, like a snow day, it needs to be a different kind of time, what some call "Time outside of time." How can you build a different kind of time into your regular routine?

TAKING IT TO THE STREET

Groups of urban pranksters have been popping up all over the world, pulling off strange and wonderful spectacles which leave onlookers puzzled or awed, or both. (For more information about this phenomenon, search online for "flash mob" or go to www.improveverywhere.com. The best flash mob I've ever seen can be viewed on the YouTube site—search for "Antwerp Do Re Mi." To see a flash mob similar to the one I'm about to propose, search for "Frozen Grand Central.")

"Daydreaming is often viewed as a sign of laziness or a lack of seriousness, but a new study says that's a bad rap. Using a magnetic resonance imaging machine to study brain activity, University of British Columbia neuroscientists found that when a person begins daydreaming, there's a lot of activity in regions of gray matter dedicated to high-level thought and complex problem-solving. 'People assume that when the mind wanders away it just gets turned off,' researcher Kalina Christoff tells LiveScience.com. 'But we show the opposite, that when it wanders, it turns on. . . . Your mind may be taking that time to address more important questions in your life.'"

—"Daydreaming Is Good for You," *The Week Magazine*, May 29, 2009

To take this lesson about the Sabbath to the streets, set a time for a large group (50-100 people or more) to take a five-minute nap in a busy public place (city square, college quad, etc.). Make sure it's at lunch time or some other busy time. Ask participants to come separately or in small groups to the location at the designated time, and act naturally, eating, or chatting on cell phones (don't all turn up as a group). It will be most effective and most mystifying for onlookers if it seems that a group of strangers decided suddenly, and by chance, to all take a nap at the same time. At a designated time, have everyone start finding a comfy spot and snooze. For added comic effect, invite participants to bring a prop—a teddy, a small pillow or blanket—which they pull out at the right time. If you want, put up signs such as "Slow Down," "Take a Break," or "Take Your Own Sweet Time" to encourage onlookers to incorporate a little Sabbath into their day (and also to be sure that onlookers don't think there's been a mass murder). Another caution: advise participants not to bring any valuables—a purse at the feet of a sleeping person might be more temptation than some can bear! Have someone set a timer or alarm clock for five minutes and when it rings, everyone can stretch, yawn, and go on their merry ways. Plan ahead to have someone secretly film or photograph the event, being sure to catch the expressions on the faces of passersby.

'Come to me, all you who are weary & burdened, & I will give you rest."
Matt 11:28

So there remains a Sabbath rest for the people of God. For the one who has entered His rest has also rested from his works as God did from His. Therefore let us be diligent to enter that rest. Heb 4

The industrial economy, by definition, must never rest.... To rest, we are persuaded, we must 'get away.' But getting away involves us in the haste, speed, & noise of escape.... there is no escape from escape. Or there is none unless we adopt the paradoxical & radical expedient of just stopping.... Biblical tradition elevates just stopping above physiological necessity, makes it a requirement, makes it an observance of the greatest dignity & mystery & assigns it a day."
LIVING THE SABBATH
Norman Wirzba

Do we truly believe ourselves children of God & members of Christ & able to rest in God & be renewed?

In the Sabbath we confront death in 2 ways—an achron ... that the ... death ... without us & a chance to ...
Peter Scazzero

WORSHIP/SERVICE

"Offer your bodies as living sacrifices, holy and pleasing to God—
this is your spiritual act of worship."
—Romans 12:1

My job means I never get to worship, or so I was told. It's my responsibility every Sunday to help others worship by overseeing the soundboard, the musicians, the PowerPoint presentation, the seating, the bulletins, the communion cups. No time for singing or sitting or listening. No worship for me.

As part of this job, I got a subscription to *Worship Leader Magazine* and, flipping through it, I became convinced of something we all already know: "Worship Leader" has come to be synonymous with "Music Minister." Out of the fifty-one advertisements in the magazine, twenty-nine were about instruments, CDs, or songs—that is, about music. We all know worship isn't just music. Every time we have a sermon series about worship, we remind people that it's not just about singing. But then the rest of the year we go back to calling our song sets "worship sets," our musicians "worship leaders."

Yes, worship *can* be music, *but could it be more?*

In a small group the discussion turned to moments we've felt most worshipful and each person shared amazing experiences of feeling God's presence. We noted afterwards how few of them happened during a church service and how many of them were breathtaking, once-in-a-lifetime kinds of experiences.

Yes, worship *can* be a euphoric experience, but could it be even more?

Many of our biblical cues for worship come from David, the exuberant dancer and musician. And so, it's only natural that we have learned that worship is music and elation and emotion. But what would worship look like if, in addition to David's approach, we got some worship cues from Paul?

Paul doesn't talk a lot about worship but when he does, he often does it in the context of the Jewish tradition, in discussions about circumcision and sacrifices. Which makes sense, since the Old Testament sense of worship had a good deal to do with sacrifice. As worshippers brought sacrifices from their fields and flocks, they brought together everyday life and spiritual practices, bringing the products of daily work into sacred space. Unfortunately, in our contemporary setting, we have divided worship from daily life. However in Romans 12:1, Paul provides a new pattern for worship (new for first-century believers and new for us): "Therefore, I urge you, brothers, in view of God's mercy, to offer your bodies as living sacrifices, holy and pleasing to God—*this is your spiritual act of worship.*" Instead of offering dead animals, we are now to offer up our living selves, more valuable to God because they carry on, allowing us to offer ongoing acts of sacrifice.

> ## RECIPE FOR A MESS
>
> I find a lot of comfort in repetitive tasks. They seem to set up a rhythm to order my thoughts. So whether it's sweeping or knitting or walking or chopping, I have found God in the mundane tasks of life.
>
> —M. S.

Paul goes on, in Romans 12, to describe the various gifts and functions of the members of the body, putting a very practical spin on worship. For him it is not only bowing and singing weekly, but serving, teaching, encouraging, contributing financially, leading, and

Worship Service

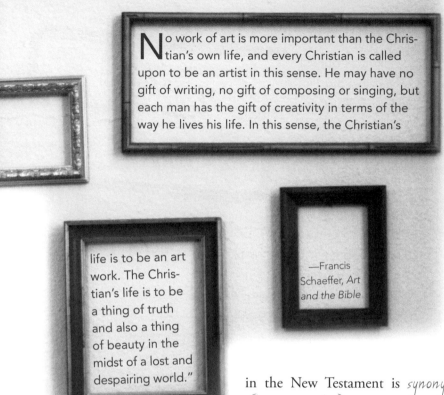

> No work of art is more important than the Christian's own life, and every Christian is called upon to be an artist in this sense. He may have no gift of writing, no gift of composing or singing, but each man has the gift of creativity in terms of the way he lives his life. In this sense, the Christian's life is to be an art work. The Christian's life is to be a thing of truth and also a thing of beauty in the midst of a lost and despairing world."

—Francis Schaeffer, *Art and the Bible*

showing mercy daily (12:6-8). In fact, the word used for worship in this passage is related to work and is often translated "service." (Sourced from K. Hess, "Latreuo," *New International Dictionary of New Testament Theology*. See other uses of various forms of the same Greek word and how it has been translated in John 16:2; Romans 9:4; Hebrews 9:1, 6; Philippians 3:3.) If worship in the Old Testament was largely synonymous with sacrifice, worship in the New Testament is *synonymous with service (living sacrifice)*, inside and outside of *the* service.

But we've got ourselves into the habit of squeezing worship into an hour and into a building. If worship is supposed to be unceasing, a way of life, then the weekly service is one of many occasions to worship. The Sunday service is special and significant, not because it's our opportunity to worship, but because it's a joint celebration of the worship that has been going on all week long, an occasion to remember the reason for the work and a time of preparation for the Monday-to-Saturday service in the week to come.

All this may explain why I love my job, why it doesn't bother me that I don't get to "worship." For me, last Sunday's service meant moving chairs, making extra copies of the bulletin, picking up trash, turning down the lights, turning up the lights, and making some announcements. I didn't get to sit. I didn't do much singing. And I almost missed out on Communion. But I've

Worship

Service

never worshiped so much in my whole life. I've never worshiped so *hard* my whole life. It's exhilarating and exhausting, just like the rest of my "worship" as wife, mother, and writer. But that's what living sacrifice feels like. This is not about changing what we're doing but acknowledging that what we're already doing is worship, if we devote it to God. There's music and there's euphoria at times, but there's also small daily choices of service, simple acts of selfless love and perseverance—lots of perseverance. It's the kind of worship that makes you sweat, the kind that means you'll need a nap this afternoon. That's what worship/service looks like. And I wouldn't go back to sitting in a pew for all the world.

"If anyone would come after me, he must deny himself and take up his cross daily and follow me. For whoever wants to save his life will lose it, but whoever loses his life for me will save it."
—Luke 9: 23, 24

Note: This essay was adapted from my article "Worship/Service: A Conversation Between Paul and David," The Christian Standard, (January 27, 2008), 13-15.

TAKE A MOMENT

1. Since Paul charges us to present our bodies and our lives as acts of worship, consider: What is your life? What is your body? Is it talents, energy, time, health, money, job, family, home?

2. However you define your body and life, how can you give them in living sacrifice?

3. Remember the times when you have served in the hardest, most sacrificial ways. Was there a sense of worship in it? How are you planning to serve God or your family or your community today? How can you make it an act of worship?

4. This is also an opportunity to raise the question of why we worship. Should we do it to get a buzz? Is worship something we consume? Can worship be an act of sacrifice, something we give, something that wears us out?

Elements of Making and Meeting

SPREADING THE MOVEMENT

"Be wise in the way you act toward outsiders; make the most of every opportunity."
—Colossians 4:5

For two years I was part of a small group which looked like a rock band. Since we played together every week, we started to function like a small group, praying and living life together. But we had a challenge: while the church was blessed with guitarists and vocalists galore, there wasn't a drummer to be found. One of the band members, who knew the local music scene, suggested that he invite the drummer from his band to join us. So Doug, whose gigs in the past were mostly in bars, was introduced to the world of The Worship Band. And, like everyone else, he became part of the group. When his wife had a miscarriage, we bore it with him and somewhere along the way, he found himself believing. But after a while, he got a new job and left town and so he sent a friend from his bar band days. This guy turned up late and groggy most Sundays, but we loved him through it and before we knew it, he was asking to be baptized. As we watched these drummers being transformed, we began to joke about the Holy Spirit dwelling in the drum kit. But it did make me think.

If it is true that our bodies can help us learn about spiritual things and if it is true that we can express worship through doing, how can a hands-on approach even work for reaching out to those who do not have a relationship with Christ? In most churches, you have to be a member before you can serve. In fact, often you have to be not only a member, but a mature Christian. Certainly, it's a valid requirement for roles of leadership, mentoring, and teaching, but are there service roles that could be OK for newcomers, even nonbelievers? It seems strange that someone who doesn't yet know Christ might want to take part in serving him, but if the church, at its heart, is a serving community, couldn't the experience of serving reveal the true heart, the true fellowship of Christ and our community? More so than a hundred newcomer lunches or outreach crusades, the experience of serving among Christ's people may show others what it means to belong to him and to us.

> Sometimes I feel I spend half of my day in the kitchen preparing, saving, and cleaning up meals. I often connect with God by asking him to partner with me in the preparation of meals. I pray for his love and blessing to flow through the food I serve to family and friends, and that the meals we share together would be a time of connection and draw us closer to each other and to God.
>
> —L. B.
>
> RECIPE FOR A MESS

TAKE A MOMENT

1. How can hands-on experiences and hard work help develop spiritual maturity in new believers? How could volunteering/serving provide opportunities for new believers, old believers, and even nonbelievers?

2. Often when we have houseguests, the guests are more comfortable when we let them wash the dishes or help out in some other way. How can we reach out to the world by, in addition to serving it, allowing them to get a preview of what it would mean to be part of the family of the church?

3. Have you ever been involved in service with others who had different beliefs about God from yours? What did you learn from that experience? If you haven't had such an experience, where could you look for such opportunities?

Making It Yours

RESOURCES TO DEVELOP YOUR OWN EXPERIMENTS

The experiments throughout this book are only some examples of ways to creatively connect with, learn about, and express love for (or frustration with) God. I hope that they have given you permission to explore the ways that work best for you. Consider the experiments which you found most helpful or meaningful. What made them so? Could you explore other ways to use those methods in your worship life?

When developing your own experiments, it may help to know a few things about yourself.

WHAT'S YOUR PLAY PERSONALITY?

In his book, *Play: How It Shapes the Brain, Opens the Imagination and Invigorates the Soul*, Stuart Brown lists the eight play personalities. I've summarized them here for you to consider your favorites. As you read, try to remember the ways you played as a child. Could it be that you still need to play in those ways?

- **The Joker:** Play usually revolves around nonsense, silly noises, being foolish.

- **The Kinesthete:** Play is movement. Kinesthetes need to move to think.

- **The Explorer:** Play is exploring, whether by literally going to new places or emotionally searching for new depths or mentally discovering new experiences.

- **The Competitor:** Play means games with specific rules where one can be the best.

- **The Director:** Play involves planning and executing scenes and events.

- **The Collector:** Collecting is play, whether it's collecting items or experiences.

- **The Artist/Creator:** Play brings joy through making anything from the fine arts to gardening, home decorating, or even fixing a bike.

- **The Storyteller:** Play occurs through either telling stories (through writing or performing), enjoying stories (through watching movies or reading), or making a story out of ordinary activities.

WHAT'S YOUR LEARNING STYLE?

Education professionals categorize learning styles in a variety of ways but they all agree that people learn differently and have different kinds of intelligences. Here is a list commonly used by educators (sourced from Lynne Celli Sarasin, *Learning Style Perspectives: Impact in the Classroom*). Note how these are connected to the play personalities. To discover your learning style(s), do the free online quiz at www.learning-styles-online.com/inventory/.

- **Logical/Mathematical:** ability to calculate, quantify, consider propositions and hypotheses, and do complex mathematical operations.
- **Linguistic:** ability to think in words and to use language to express and appreciate complex meanings.
- **Musical:** sensitivity to pitch, rhythm, and tone.
- **Spatial:** capacity to think in three-dimensional ways, to perceive imagery, to modify images, to move oneself or objects through space, and to understand how objects are related and how they fit together in an ordered manner.
- **Bodily/Kinesthetic:** ability to manipulate objects and fine-tune physical skills.
- **Interpersonal:** capacity to understand and interact effectively with other people.
- **Intrapersonal:** ability to construct an accurate perception of oneself and to use such knowledge in planning and directing one's life.

WHAT'S YOUR LOVE LANGUAGE?

Counselor Gary Chapman's best-selling books detail the five basic ways we give and recognize love (*The Five Love Languages*). We may be "multilingual" but when it comes to discovering how we express our feelings to

God, it may help us to consider how we express our feelings to others through exploring these five love languages. To read more and do an assessment, go to www.5lovelanguages.com.

⊛ words of affirmation　⊛ quality time

⊛ receiving gifts　⊛ acts of service　⊛ physical touch

BUILDING COMMUNITY EVENTS

If you want to develop your own community experiments, check out some of these for inspiration:

- Carol Ann Newsome's New Leaf Project (www.newleaf.carolannnewsome.com)

- Amy Krouse Rosenthal posted "17 things I made" on YouTube, inviting people to join her on 8/08/08 at a park in Chicago to make an 18th thing together. She was surprised to find hundreds of people met her there and "The Beckoning of Lovely" is the video of what happened.

- Park(ing) Day (www.parkingday.org)

- 1,000 Journals Project—www.1000journals.com and the book, *1000 Journals Project* by Someguy and Kevin Kelly

- Improv Everywhere (www.improveverywhere.com) and their book, *Causing a Scene: Extraordinary Pranks in Ordinary Places with Improv Everywhere* by Charlie Todd and Alex Scordelis

God created the world and infused it with his spirit. He gave us bodies and senses so that we could enjoy it—and find him in it. But finding and fathoming God is a lifelong process—an individual and shared one. It requires faith and patience. And it thrives on openness, playfulness, and creativity.

So go.
　　Make a mess.
　　　　God is waiting to meet you there.

Bibliography and Resources

Works cited in this book

Ball, Philip. *Bright Earth: Art and the Invention of Color*. Chicago: University of Chicago Press, 2001, vii.

Bonhoeffer, Dietrich. *The Cost of Discipleship*. New York: Touchstone, 1995, 92.

Book of Common Prayer. Cambridge: University Press.

Boyink, Michael. "Seeing God in the Mess." Accessed at http://www.storiesaboutgod.org/index.php/stories/story_page/seeing-god-in-the-mess/.

Briñol, Pablo and Richard E. Petty. "Overt Head Movements and Persuasion: A Self-Evaluation Analysis" *Journal of Personality and Social Psychology*. 2003, Vol. 84, No. 6.

Brother Lawrence. *The Brother Lawrence Collection: Practice and Presence of God, Spiritual Maxims, the Life of Brother Lawrence*. Wilder Publications, 2008, 23, 56.

Brown, Stuart with Christopher Vaughan. *Play: How It Shapes the Brain, Opens the Imagination, and Invigorates the Soul*. New York: Penguin Books, 2009, 66–70, 84, 218.

Burns, Marilyn. *The Book of Think: Or How to Solve a Problem Twice Your Size* (A Brown Paper School Book). Canada: Little, Brown & Co. (Juv), 1976.

Burns, Paul. *Butler's Lives of the Saints*. Minnesota: Liturgical Press, 2003, 345.

Chapman, Gary. *The Five Love Languages: How to Express Heartfelt Commitment to Your Mate*. Chicago: Northfield Publishing, 1992.

Collins, John J. *The Apocalyptic Imagination: An Introduction to the Jewish Apocalyptic Literature*. Grand Rapids, MI: Wm. B. Eerdmans Publishing Co., 1998, 5.

Davidson, Rosemary. *Take a Look: An Introduction to the Experience of Art*. New York: Viking, 1993, 13.

"Daydreaming Is Good for You," *The Week Magazine*. May 29, 2009.

Edwards, Betty. *The New Drawing on the Right Side of the Brain: A Course in Enhancing Creativity and Artistic Confidence*. New York: Tarcher/Putnam, 1999.

Erikson, Joan M. *Wisdom and the Senses: The Way of Creativity*. New York: W. W. Norton and Co., 1988, 65, 67–8.

Ferlo, Roger. *Sensing God: Reading Scripture with All Our Senses*. Cambridge, MA: Cowley Publications, 2002, 6–7.

Foster, Richard. *Prayer: Finding the Heart's True Home*. New York: Harper Collins, 1992, xii.

Foucault, Michel. *Ethics: Subjectivity and Truth*. New York: The New Press, 1997, 208.

Frayling, Christophe, Helen Frayling, and Ron Van Der Meer. *The Art Pack*. London: Ebury, 1992.

Garrett, Steven. "Warner Herzog Walks the Rope." *Esquire Magazine*, September, 2008, 52.

Gogh, Vincent van. Irving Stone, ed. *Dear Theo: The Autobiography of Vincent van Gogh*. New York: Plume Publishing, 1995, 277.

Hatfield, Elaine, John T. Cacioppo, and Richard L. Rapson. *Emotional Contagion*. Cambridge: Cambridge University Press, 1994, 66.

Henry, Patrick. *The Ironic Christian's Companion: Finding the Marks of God's Grace in the World*. New York: Riverhead Books, 2000, 7.

Hess, K. "Latreuo," *New International Dictionary of New Testament Theology*. Colin Brown, ed. Zondervan, Pradis 5.0, 2002.

James, Jamie. *The Music of the Spheres: Music, Science and the Natural Order of the Universe*. New York: Springer-Verlag, 1993, 145.

Lakoff, George and Mark Johnson. *Philosophy in the Flesh: The Embodied Mind and Its Challenge to Western Thought*. New York: Basic Books, 1999, 564, 567.

Lewis, C. S. *Letters to Malcolm: Chiefly on Prayer*. Orlando, Florida: Harvest Books, 2002, 4.

Lewis, C. S. *The Screwtape Letters*. New York: Harper Collins, 2001, 40.

Lowry, Robert. "How Can I Keep from Singing?" 1860. Words taken from The Cyber Hymnal, http://nethymnal.org/htm/h/c/hcaikeep.htm.

Niebuhr, Reinhold. "The Serenity Prayer," from *Living the Serenity Prayer*, James Stuart Bell and Jeanette Gardner Littleton, eds. Avon, MA: Adams Media, 2008, 3.

Noë, Alva. *Out of Our Heads: Why You Are Not Your Brain, and Other Lessons from the Biology of Consciousness*. New York: Hill and Wang, 2009, xii.

Nouwen, Henri. *Can You Drink the Cup?* Notre Dame, IN: Ave Maria Press, 2006, 42.

Oech, Roger von. *A Kick in the Seat of the Pants: Using Your Explorer, Artist, Judge and Warrior to Be More Creative*. California: Harper Perennial, 1986, 86.

O'Regan, Colette. "I Am Poem." Submitted by Colette Buckley. *Voices* Online Edition, Vol. XXIV, No. 1. Women for Faith and Family. Eastertide 2009.

Reynolds, Peter. *Ish*. Massachusetts: Candlewick, 2004.

Robinson, Edward. *The Language of Mystery*. Philadelphia: Trinity Press International, 1989, 25, 37.

Sarasin, Lynne Celli. *Learning Style Perspectives: Impact in the Classroom*. Madison, WI: Atwood Publications, 1998, 3–4.

Scazzero, Peter. From his Urban Monasticism workshop, CCDA Conference, 2008.

Schaeffer, Francis A. *Art and the Bible*. Downers Grove, IL: InterVarsity Press, 1973.

Schaeffer, Franky. *Addicted to Mediocrity: 20th Century Christians and the Arts*. Illinois: Crossway Books, 1982.

Smith, Mandy. *Life Is Too Important to Be Taken Seriously: Kite-Flying Lessons from Ecclesiastes*. Joplin, MO: College Press, 2004.

Spafford, Horatio G. "It Is Well with My Soul," 1873. Words taken from The Cyber Hymnal, http://nethymnal.org/htm/i/t/i/itiswell.htm.

Striker, Susan. *The Anti-Coloring Book*. New York: Henry Holt and Company, 1984, Introduction.

Thompson, Dr. Tom. Said in conversation with author.

Thoreau, Henry David. *A Week on the Concord and Merrimack Rivers/ Walden; Or, Life in the Woods/ The Maine Woods/ Cape Cod*. New York: Penguin Putnam, 1985, 238.

Truitt, Anne. *Daybook: The Journal of an Artist*. New York: Penguin Books, 1982, 44.

Wilde, Oscar. *Complete Works of Oscar Wilde*. New York: Harper and Row, 1989, 390, 665.

Wilkinson, Francis. Editorial. *The Week Magazine*. July 31, 2009. Vol. 9, Issue 423.

Willard, Dallas. *The Divine Conspiracy: Rediscovering Our Hidden Life in God*. San Francisco: Harper Collins, 1998, 14.

Winner, Lauren. *Mudhouse Sabbath: An Invitation to a Life of Spiritual Discipline*. Brewster, MA: Paraclete Press, 2007, ix–x.

Other resources

Bass, Alice. *The Creative Life: A Workbook for Unearthing the Christian Imagination*.

Bustard, Ned, ed. *It Was Good: Making Art to the Glory of God*.

Dawtry, Anne and Christopher Irvine. *Art and Worship*.

Dyrness, William A. *Visual Faith: Art, Theology, and Worship in Dialogue* (Engaging Culture).

Elsheimer, Janice. *The Creative Call: An Artist's Response to the Way of the Spirit*.

Ferguson, George. *Signs & Symbols in Christian Art*.

Finlay, Victoria. *Color: A Natural History of the Palette*.

Generate Magazine. www.generatemagazine.wordpress.com

Jensen, Robin M. *The Substance of Things Seen: Art, Faith, and the Christian Community* (Calvin Institute of Christian Worship Liturgical Studies).

Lansingh, Steve, ed. "Film Forum: Recognizing Art as Worship." *Christianity Today* online. www.christianitytoday.com/ct/2000/marchweb-only/12.0.html

L'Engle, Madeleine. *Walking on Water: Reflections on Faith and Art.*

Neighbors Abbey. www.neighborsabbey.org

Scott, Steve. *Like a House on Fire: Renewal of the Arts in a Postmodern Culture.*

Turner, Steve. *Imagine: A Vision for Christians in the Arts.*

Veith, Gene Edward. *State of the Arts: From Bezalel to Mapplethorpe* (Turning Point Christian Worldview Series).

Viladesau, Richard. *Theology and the Arts: Encountering God Through Music, Art, and Rhetoric.*

Wuthnow, Robert. *All in Sync: How Music and Art Are Revitalizing American Religion.*

Churches and programs to check out

Austin Stone Community Church, Austin, Texas. www.austinstone.org

Calvin Institute of Christian Worship, Grand Rapids, Michigan. www.calvin.edu/worship/

Church As Art blog. www.ChurchAsArt.com/blog/

Ecclesia Church, Houston, Texas. www.ecclesiahouston.org

Journey, Dallas, Texas. www.journeydallas.com

Mosaic, Austin, Texas. www.mosaicaustin.org

Scottsdale Congregational United Church of Christ, Scottsdale, Arizona. www.artinworship.com

Sojourn Community Church, Louisville, Kentucky. www.sojournchurch.com

UBC, Waco, Texas. www.ubc.org

University Christian Church, Cincinnati, Ohio. www.universitychristianchurch.net

Bible References Index

Items marked in **bold** are the readings for the Experiments.

Themes Index

About the Author

Australian-born Mandy Smith is an artist, author, pastor, and speaker. She has spent the past twenty years living and ministering in Britain and the U.S. Her current ministry is focused on her work as an Associate Pastor at University Christian Church, a church founded in 1989 to serve the University of Cincinnati (Ohio) community.

A regular speaker at conferences and church events, Mandy's other written works include *Life Is Too Important to Be Taken Seriously: Kite-Flying Lessons from Ecclesiastes* (College Press). As one of her many artistic outlets, Mandy is also the creator and coordinator of a city-wide art-from-trash project, The Collect, for which she was named one of Cincinnati's Coolest People by *CityBeat* magazine.

Mandy resides in the city with her husband and their two children.

About the Cover

The cover for *Making a Mess and Meeting God* was the inspiration and work of Scott Ryan, who is a senior designer at Standard Publishing. After several conversations with the author and a trip to her home to delve into her collections of found objects, Scott came away with an idea to create a physical piece of art that would embody some of the thoughts conveyed by Mandy Smith's writing. He also gained inspiration from the kind of craftsmanship and experimentation talked about in a book by Michael de Meng, *Secrets of Rusty Things*.

Bit by bit the things that were just random pieces of refuse came together to create an artistic metaphor for the book's main message: that ordinary—even broken—parts of life can, with a little faith, patience, and playfulness, come together to make something hopeful and meaningful, something that connects us with God. "The connections are uncanny," said Scott, who mainly chose pieces at random for their look and feel, rather than for any spiritual significance. Nevertheless, at the completion of the work, the biblical metaphors came to light: a battered salt shaker lid for the salt of the world, twisted wire that brings to mind the thorny crown, rusty nails for the nails of the cross, a saw blade for the carpenter's Son, leaves of a cuckoo clock that hint at God's eternal nature, and a camera lens that reminds us that "Now we see through a glass, darkly, but then face to face." Author Mandy Smith said, "It's like all the words in the book got together to create the cover art."

The piece of art was exhibited at the Rohs Street Café in Cincinnati, Ohio, throughout the season of Lent, 2010. For his part, Scott hopes others who see the piece or the cover image are able to find connections in it and be inspired to make their own creations: to take worthless things and make something out of them.